25 Practical Uses for Radical Forgiveness

A Handbook for Solving the Problems and Challenges of Everyday Life in a New Way

COLIN C. TIPPING

25 Practical Uses for Radical Forgiveness: *A Handbook for Solving the Problems and Challenges of Everyday Life in a New Way*

Published in Spring, 2014

Printed in the United States of America

ISBN 978-0-9821790-3-1

Global 13 Publications, Inc.
355 Ridge Hill Circle,
Marietta GA 30064
info@radicalforgiveness.com

Website: www.radicalforgiveness.com
Cover Design: Colin Tipping and Shari Claire
Illustrations: Ken Shearer
Editing: Kathy Henry
Proof Reading: Karla Garrett
Photographs: Katie Klein, www.katieklienphotography.com

Dedicated to My Three Children,

Lorraine, Jonathan and Caroline
who have found it in their hearts to forgive me for all my
failings as a father and who love me just the way I am.

And My Grandchildren

**Daniel, Sian, Matthew, Bryony, Eleanor, Daisy,
Rosie, Alfie, Andrew and Brandon**
who may one day read this book
and understand who I was.

Acknowledgements

I wish to express my profound sense of gratitude to my team at the Institute for Radical Forgiveness and Global 13 Publications, Karla Garrett, Shari Claire, Kathy Henry and David Klosen for all their terrific support over many years. Without their help, their loyalty and their expertise, this and the other books written before this one could not have been written. Nor could JoAnn and I have been able to travel the world spreading the message of Radical Forgiveness so widely, knowing that everything back home was being taken care of. I am so blessed to have them in my life and in my business.

My appreciation also extends with love to the two people who have, with such love, supported me and the work in Europe, Hina Fruh in Germany and Margrit Hardegger in Switzerland.

I also owe a special debt of gratitude to the countless number of people who have done so much to spread the message around the world by attending workshops, recommending the work through word of mouth and, more recently, via Facebook and Twitter.

My thanks also go to all the hundreds of Radical Living Coaches and Radical Forgiveness Therapy Practitioners who are helping people everywhere heal their lives through Radical Forgiveness.

I also have to thank the wonderfully talented Karen Taylor-Good whose songs and singing add an indescribably wonderful tone to every workshop we do.

iii

Finally, I send a special 'thank you' and much love to my wife JoAnn for her unconditional love and support, for believing in me and the work, and for being willing to travel the world with me as my co-facilitator and partner. What more could one ask for?

CONTENTS

Introduction

Since developing the Radical Forgiveness process and writing the book, *Radical Forgiveness: Making Room for the Miracle* in 1997, I have taken it all around the world doing clinics, workshops and speaking tours based on this amazing technology. It has proven to be extremely effective in helping people solve a wide variety of problems that tended to get in the way of leading a happy and fulfilling life.

Up to now, however, people have tended to think of it only in terms of its power to heal the long-held grievances and wounds of the past. They failed to see how it could be applied to things that occur from time to time to most of us in our daily lives. They applied it once or twice and then never thought to use it again for other things.

As a remedy for this under-utilization of a great process for healing, this book will open peoples' eyes to the wider potential for increasing happiness by applying Radical Forgiveness and Radical Self-Forgiveness to all manner of things across the whole spectrum of human experience. Here are some examples of where it has proven to be effective.

Typical Problems Solved by Radical Forgiveness

• Relationship problems of all kinds resolved

• The pain of old hurts released (e.g. abandonment, sexual abuse, rejection, infidelity, betrayal, physical abuse, shaming, injustice, rape, incest, divorce, discrimination, etc.)

- Anger towards people who have wounded you transformed (e.g. parents, siblings, spouse, ex-spouse, partners, boss, professional service people, etc.)

- Mistreatment by institutions or organizations transformed (e.g. governments, press, churches, cults, groups, the justice system, the medical system, etc.)

- Addiction to being a victim released

- Addictions of all kinds helped

- Residual anger, blame and resentment released

- Significant body weight reduction in many cases

- Certain physical conditions healed and health improved

- Cancer — likelihood reduced or even prevented

- Inability to create success reversed

- Blocked creative power unleashed

- Inability to create a loving relationship reversed

- Poverty consciousness reversed

- Level of prosperity raised

- Patterns of self-limitation and sabotage dissolved

Typical Problems Solved by Radical SELF-Forgiveness
- Incessant self-criticism and judgment relieved

- Excessive guilt and shame released

- Low self-esteem restored to normal levels

- Injured self-respect restored

- Self-loathing transformed into self-acceptance

While these are somewhat generalized, I have chosen in this book to focus on 25 specific issues that people tend to struggle with in their lives, and to show how adopting a Radical Forgiveness perspective will help resolve them.

Besides being a reference book that enables people to direct their energies towards healing specific issues, whether they are health related, relationship specific, work centered or just about growing and learning, many of the tools required to make it work are to be found right here in the pages of the book.

However, in addition to those given in the book, I have listed at the end of each application all the tools that would be appropriate for that particular one. Each of them are then listed in the Resources Section along with instructions on how to gain access to them.

My hope is that this book they will open peoples' eyes to the wider potential for increasing happiness by applying Radical Forgiveness and Radical Self-Forgiveness to all manner of things across the whole spectrum of normal life and human experience.

Chapter 1:
Preparing the Ground

S ome readers may already be very familiar with the concept of Radical Forgiveness, but others may not. This being the case, I would like to give a brief explanation of what it is, what makes it so special, and why it is so different from conventional forgiveness. I also want you to understand why it works so very quickly when conventional forgiveness takes years.

If you are completely new to the concept and wish to go deeper into it, you might want to find a copy of my first book, *Radical Forgiveness: A Revolutionary 5-Stage Process to Heal Relationships, Let Go of Anger and Blame and Find*

Peace in Any Situation. In the meantime, the brief thumbnail sketch I am giving here will suffice.

In practice, the process of Radical Forgiveness consists of five distinct stages, the first three of which are more or less the same as conventional forgiveness. The fourth and fifth stages are where all the action is. And I should warn you – it is likely to blow your mind.

But hang in there with me because you don't have to believe it for it to work. The more skeptical you are, the better I like it! I'm skeptical too, and, like me, you will be more impressed by the results when you experience it than will someone who expected it. Anyway, let me take you through the five stages and you will see what I mean.

Stage One is where you tell the story of what happened, why you feel victimized, who is to blame and so on. Nothing unusual there.

Stage Two, which usually arises from Stage One, is to give yourself permission to feel the full range of feelings associated with the story, no matter what they are. This is an important step because you cannot heal what you don't feel. It can take a while to get into the feelings but that's OK. Just ask yourself, am I mad, sad, glad or afraid? That's a good way to start.

Stage Three asks you to take a step back. Try to understand the person's motives for doing what they did. Bring some empathy, mercy and compassion into the mix, and try to cut them some slack in spite of what they did to you. You also try to cut out all the 'extras' in the story – the stuff that isn't quite true but which you added to the story to further justify your victimhood.

6

This is as far as conventional forgiveness can go. It still identifies you as a victim. Even though you are making an effort to forgive the person, he or she is not let off the hook. He/she is still seen as a perpetrator responsible for your pain and unhappiness.

Stage Four. This is where Radical Forgiveness takes us to where few have been before. This stage asks that we make a dramatic shift in our thinking about ourselves and the world we inhabit. We call this stage the Radical Forgiveness Reframe. Get ready!

It is at this stage that Radical Forgiveness asks us to become willing to embrace a new philosophy of life and a new paradigm of reality. We are required to be open to the possibility that there is Divine purpose in everything, and that at the spiritual level there is nothing to forgive. That's because everything that occurs happens not TO us but FOR us. It's all part of our own Divine plan. Therefore, there are no mistakes. Everything happens for a reason.

Stage Five. At the beginning of the process, the energy attached to your victim story was firmly held in the cellular structure of your body. Having just done the reframe, which turns your old victim story on its head, the last task now is to replace the old victim story with the new one. This is achieved by doing something physical like 'Satori' Breathwork, dancing, chanting, writing or walking.

So, that's it in a nutshell. Is your mouth gaping open? Is your mind already thinking, "That's a stupid idea!" Why wouldn't it? It goes against everything we know to be true, doesn't it?

Even if your mind is still thinking about it, I bet it has already thought of many exceptions, right?

Of course it has. Your mind is built to question everything, to find the logical flaws in any idea. It must make sense according to its own model of reality, and clearly Radical Forgiveness does not. But I can assure you that there is another part of you that knows the Truth and totally gets it. So don't worry — even though it sounds ridiculous, the process works anyway.

I can say, with complete confidence, that it works because over the years we have found that most people who try it become profoundly changed. All their old hurts dissolve. Their long held resentments seem to just melt away. Relationships are healed. Connections get made and synchronicities occur that show them there is a different set of laws operating at some other level. Problems simply go away, and life works better.

As I say in the Afterword in my book, Radical Forgiveness, "...it is nothing less than a mind-blowing idea that shatters our existing ideas of reality and challenges our current world view. It invites us to engage in a process that is rooted in a model of reality which we don't yet understand. Neither is there much proof of its efficacy other than the evidence of our own awareness of how significantly changed we become when we engage in it."

What is Radical SELF-Forgiveness?
It would be quite right to say that Radical Self-Forgiveness is exactly the same as Radical Forgiveness, except for the fact that you are the one being forgiven. However, it is not quite as easy as that. For a start, most people agree that it is much

more difficult to forgive oneself than to forgive others, even if we do use the Radical version of self-forgiveness.

Then there is the more difficult problem of being both the forgiver and the forgiven. When we say "I forgive myself," it raises the question, *"Who's forgiving whom?"* Therein lies the root of the problem.

How this is resolved is spelled out in Application #15, "Find Love and Acceptance for Yourself, Just the Way You Are." I felt that this deserved its own application.

From this point on in the book, then, for the sake of brevity and convenience, the term Radical Forgiveness shall include Radical Self-Forgiveness and Radical Self-Acceptance. The technology with which all three are applied in the real world is known as **The Tipping Method.**

A Practical Spirituality
Radical Forgiveness is not just for healing old hurts rooted in the past. People can apply the Radical Forgiveness perspective and process to a whole range of problems and events that are all part of the tapestry of everyday life. This was the light bulb idea and the inspiration for this book, which offers many practical and down-to-earth applications for Radical Forgiveness.

I believe that unless spiritual ideas and practices have practical application to our everyday lives, they aren't much good. They need to provide a link between the two worlds, so that what we do in the world as human beings carries meaning in spiritual terms, not simply for our survival and comfort.

The other thing we have discovered is that the process of Radical Forgiveness, while it is simple and easy to do, only seems to work if you use the special tools provided. On the surface, they appear to be simple worksheets and audio equivalents, but the fact is they seem to be totally necessary.

This is because our rational minds will always have trouble with Radical Forgiveness, as it really does seem to be an 'off-the-wall' idea. The Radical Forgiveness tools – worksheets, audios, and online programs – enable us to bypass our rational minds, connecting us with our Spiritual Intelligence. We are not fully aware of this faculty of mind yet, but nevertheless our Spiritual Intelligence is activated when we use those tools. This is the part of us that is connected into Universal Intelligence. It knows who we are and why we are here. That's why the worksheets make perfect sense to it, while the rational mind likely sees them as nonsense.

Radical Forgiveness is essentially a 'fake-it-'til-you-make-it' system. The tools provide the means of faking it, because they ask only that you be *willing* to be open to the possibility that the ideas contained in the new paradigm *might* be true. That placates the rational mind and, consequently, it gives up its resistance. Your Spiritual Intelligence takes it from there.

This is the essence of the Radical Forgiveness approach. It is the thread that runs through everything in this book. It is an optimistic form of spirituality which frees us from judgment, blame, resentment, guilt and fear. At the same time, it recognizes and accepts the essential need for souls to experience such feelings as part of their spiritual advancement.

As you apply Radical Forgiveness to everyday challenges, your experience of life will change significantly for the better. You will be able to move through life in a much more peaceful and accepting manner than ever before. You will develop a greater degree of both compassion and wisdom. Your relationships will become more meaningful and enlightening. Your health will improve and you will have more energy for living.

So to recap the practical features of Radical Forgiveness and the Tipping Method it embodies, they are as follows:

a) It requires no skill or special ability. Anyone can do it, even if they are totally skeptical — it still works. One does not even have to believe in its central idea that *there are no accidents and that our soul has created the circumstances of our lives for our spiritual growth.* All it requires is a willingness to at least be open to that possibility.

b) Since it works energetically, it operates outside the parameters of time and space. Consequently, results are immediate. Distance is no factor in terms of the effect it might have energetically on all the people involved, as well as on the actual situation causing the initial upset.

c) There is no inherent conflict between the need to condemn and the desire to forgive. From a spiritual perspective, nothing wrong has happened, and there is nothing to forgive.

d) It sets one free from victim consciousness. From a spiritual perspective, there are no victims and perpetrators – just teachers and learners.

e) There is a proven step-by-step methodology inherent in Radical Forgiveness that is absent in traditional forgiveness. This methodology is called The Tipping Method, and it provides tools that give everyone the opportunity to go through one or more Radical Forgiveness processes – at anytime, anywhere and for whatever reason.

Having made a case for the practicality of Radical Forgiveness even though it seems crazy, I feel I must add another theoretical dimension to it which will make it seem even more so. Again, you don't have to believe it.

For those who, like me, appreciate a 'left-brained' model of how things might work on which to hang a concept, here's one you might like. It is based on my observations of people in my workshops over the years, and answers some of the questions raised by the Radical Forgiveness paradigm. Such questions include:

Why are we here?
Why take on a human body and
come to this earth plane?
Why incarnate at all?
What is the purpose?

What follows is my take on it. I don't know whether it is 'the Truth,' but it seems to resonate with a lot of people when I present it to them. It just seems to feel right. It goes like this.

I think it is likely that souls are still in the process of evolving, even in the spiritual realm, and that at some moment in the soul's evolution it will begin seeking the true meaning of its own existence in the presence of Love and Light. It will also develop a desire to know what it really means to be in the state of Oneness. But the only way the soul can know these things is to experience the opposite of them: darkness, fear and separation.

Yet, just to know them would not be enough. They would want to experience each of them as a feeling, and for that they would need a body. So they would lower their vibration and incarnate as a human being on the earth plane. Their soul's journey as a spiritual being having a human experience would begin there.

However, in order for them to have the full emotional experience of being separate, fearful and in darkness, they would have to submit to having spiritual amnesia for a certain number of years.

They would need to believe that this human reality is the one reality, and that the life they begin to live as a human being is the only life. Otherwise they wouldn't play the game as it was meant to be played.

But having signed up for a certain amount of pain of separation, fear and darkness, measured in what I call karmic units, they would subconsciously create as many opportunities as possible through which to feel the pain of separation.

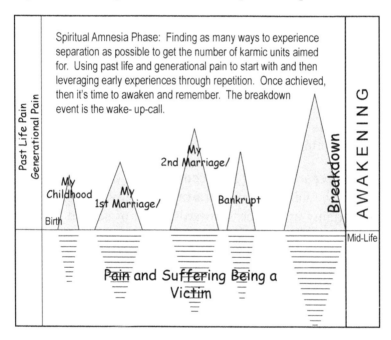

Fig. 1: The Soul's Journey (1)

Once they experience the amount of fear, darkness and separation they signed up for, they would begin the process of awakening and remembering who they are. My observation is that this tends to happen around midway through life.

In case you are wondering where you are in your own soul's journey, my assessment is that, irrespective of your age, you would not be reading this book if you were not either at or beyond that point of awakening. If not, you would have put this book down a long time ago. You would still have too many more karmic units yet to gather before this idea was revealed to you.

So, assuming we have awakened, having had as much experience of separation as we needed, we can now go back along the time line of our lives and, using Radical Forgiveness, begin clearing away the debris of our traumas, our old belief systems, our mistakes, our disasters and everything else that served its purpose during the spiritual amnesia phase. It is now just toxic energy waiting to be dumped.

This prepares us for the second phase of our life, during which we shift our concerns away from survival, competition, materiality and success towards being of service to others, staying awake, healing ourselves and saving the planet.

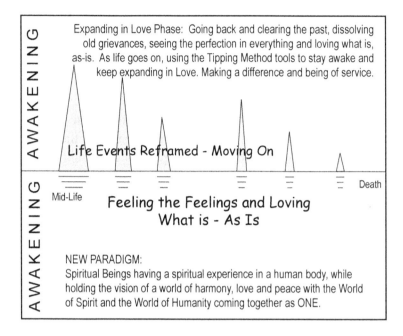

Expanding in Love Phase: Going back and clearing the past, dissolving old grievances, seeing the perfection in everything and loving what is, as-is. As life goes on, using the Tipping Method tools to stay awake and keep expanding in Love. Making a difference and being of service.

AWAKENING

Life Events Reframed - Moving On

Mid-Life

Death

Feeling the Feelings and Loving What is - As Is

AWAKENING

NEW PARADIGM:
Spiritual Beings having a spiritual experience in a human body, while holding the vision of a world of harmony, love and peace with the World of Spirit and the World of Humanity coming together as ONE.

Fig. 2: The Soul's Journey (2)

So that's it. I refer to it as the Soul's Journey. It is explained in more detail in my book, *Getting to Heaven on a Harley,* and in *Expanding into Love*, but hopefully this is sufficient to provide the context for what follows in this book. If nothing else, when I speak of the Awakening, you will know what I mean.

But again, let me stress: Belief is not necessary. As I said before, Radical Forgiveness is a fake-it-til-you-make-it process anyway. It happens in spite of you.

POSTSCRIPT

As mentioned earlier, if you are relatively new to the concept or would like to delve deeper into the core ideas, you will find reading the book *Radical Forgiveness* very helpful. I would also recommend *Getting to Heaven on a Harley.*

Most of what you will find in this book, and all the tools and programs referenced in the Resources Section at the back of the book, are designed as self-help tools. Though Radical Forgiveness is a healing modality it is designed for people who are basically well and have a desire to solve the problems of everyday life and to bring more peace and contentment.

However, if you have picked up this book because you are in severe emotional pain and are looking for immediate relief at this time, then please go to our website, www. radicalforgiveness.com, and find a Radical Forgiveness Practitioner who will provide one-on-one support for you. They will take you through the process and give you the kind of extra support you need. Don't let it slide. Do it now!

Chapter 3:
Ditching Victim Consciousness

Victim consciousness is a highly toxic and totally disempowering belief system. It can be defined as the conviction that someone has done something 'bad' to you and, as a direct result, they are entirely responsible for the lack of peace and happiness in your life.

As long as you feel others are responsible for your life and for your happiness, you remain stuck. If you don't rise above this way of thinking it will draw you back into more of the same stuff you created (then for good purpose) earlier on.

Victim consciousness is very seductive. When something bad happens and you get upset it is extremely easy for you to forget everything you ever knew about Radical Forgiveness and go straight back to 'Victimland.' Looking at the diagram below you will see the problem is that once you go there, you tend to stay there for a very long time. Without a Radical Forgiveness viewpoint, you would probably stay there for years, which is what most people do.

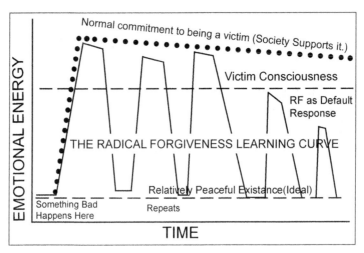

Fig. 3: *The Victimland Roller Coaster*

However, should someone who understands Radical Forgiveness and recognizes your symptoms suggest you do a worksheet or listen to the 13 Steps CD you may find yourself having returned to peace.

Alternatively, you can use the Emerge-n-See 4-Step Process right there in the moment to stop yourself going to Victimland. All you do is say the following steps to yourself:

1. Look what I've created.
2. I notice my judgments and feelings but love myself anyway.
3. I am willing to see the perfection in the situation.
4. I choose peace.

As soon as you find yourself getting upset over something, or even if you find yourself making judgments, feeling self-righteous, or wanting to change something about a situation, use this 4-step process, and/or one of the other Tipping Method Tools to bring your consciousness back into alignment with the principles of Radical Forgiveness.

However, before you can release victim consciousness you must fully grasp one key metaphysical concept. This is, *we are 100% responsible for whatever shows up in our lives.* Everything 'out-there' is a reflection of our own consciousness. We create our reality with our thoughts, feelings, beliefs and imagination. (See Step One of the 4-Step Process above.)

This happens through the natural law known as the Law of Attraction. Whatever we conceive and give power to with our mind will manifest. This law is neutral and does not judge. It simply responds to whatever energy you put out and cares not whether it is good or bad, positive or negative. It just manifests in form what you put out as thought and emotion. You are the one who chooses its value.

Some things are created in this way by individuals, others by groups while the big stuff is created through mass consciousness. There are no exceptions and I can say that because the quantum physicists say exactly the same thing: "Consciousness is the creative element in the universe."

Renowned physicist David Bohm claims that the tangible reality of everyday life is really just an illusion, no more than just a holographic image. Beneath the so-called 'objective' reality lies a deeper order of reality that continually gives birth to the material world. He called this level of reality the *implicate order* in which things that are not yet manifest are "**en**folded," just waiting to be made manifest (**un**folded) through the mechanism of consciousness. When consciousness causes this to occur it becomes 'explicate' and forms what Bohm calls the *explicate order* of reality.

To Bohm, the manifestation of all form is simply the result of innumerable shifts between the implicate and explicate order of reality. There is no limit to what can be made explicate out of the implicate order. It's all in there, enfolded in the implicate order in the form of energy, just waiting for us to bring it forth and make it explicate through our consciousness.

Therefore the question arises: Do we want to manifest our reality with **conscious intention** now that we are awake? Or are we content to continue creating it unconsciously according to the crappy habitual thoughts, feelings and beliefs we have been projecting out there in the past? They may have satisfied our need for separation but they no longer need do so. Consequently, we need to send them to the graveyard of ideas.

By the way, while in the Introduction I spoke only of the individual soul's journey and its awakening, I firmly believe that we are on the cusp of the awakening of the whole of humanity. When that happens we will all be operating from the new paradigm characterized by Radical Forgiveness. There will be no further need for separation because Oneness will be the operating principle underlying everything.

Right now it looks like we are going through the period of breakdown that always seems to precede a mass shift in consciousness. This is so we can see the world we have created by our imaginings up to now, realize it to be an illusion and create a whole new world.

In the new paradigm there are no victims or perpetrators. We understand we are all here in service to each other by providing opportunities to experience separation. In many instances what we experience here as painful was pre-arranged as part of a soul contract.

This constitutes the afore-mentioned 4th step in the Radical Forgiveness process - the Reframe. Neale Donald Walsch wrote a very nice parable to explain this to children. The book was called *The Little Soul and the Sun*. With all due apologies to Neale, here is a very shortened adaptation of the story:

THE LITTLE SOUL STORY
There once was a little soul who declared to God,

"I know who I am!"

God replied, "You do? Who are you?"

"I am the Light," *shouted the little soul,* **"and it's really cool!"**

"But, you know God – just _knowing_ I am the light is not enough. I want to _experience_ myself as the light." cried the little soul.

"Okay." God said, "We can arrange that, no problem. But, if you want to truly experience yourself as the light, we'll just surround you with darkness first so you will know the difference."

"But will I be afraid of the dark?" asked the little soul, rather nervously.

"Oh no," said God, "We're only pretending. But I have just the place for you. It's called Planet Earth. And I have lots of angels down there who will give you the chance to experience the darkness in the roles they will play for you — just so you can discern the difference and remember who you are."

"That sounds cool," said the little soul.

"Yes, it is." said God. "You'll be amazed at the kinds of tricks I put people up to – some I ask to play being mean and nasty, while I ask others to be really kind, loving and generous. It's just a game, really, and all of them are angels, of course, but it enables everyone in the end to experience themselves as the light."

"Well, when I go down there, I want you to give me the job of demonstrating forgiveness," said the little soul. "I want to experience myself as one who forgives!"

"Oh, sure," said God. "But there's a bit of a problem with that, though."

"What?" cried the little soul, a little impatiently.

"There's no one to forgive," said God quietly.

"No one!" cried the little soul in astonishment.

"No one," repeated God. "You see, everyone is perfect. Everyone is doing exactly what they need to be doing. There is not a single soul in all creation less perfect than you. Look around."

Looking at the large crowd of souls that had gathered, the Little Soul had to agree. They were all absolutely perfect.

"Who, then, to forgive?" asked God.

"Boy, this is going to be no fun at all!" grumbled the little soul. "I wanted to experience myself as One Who Forgives." And the Little Soul learned what it must feel like to be sad.

But just then a Friendly Soul stepped forward from the crowd.

"Not to worry, Little Soul. I will help you."

25

'You will?" the little soul brightened.
"But what can you do?"

"Why, I can give you someone to forgive!"

"You can?"

"Certainly!" chirped the Friendly Soul, "I can come down to
Earth with you and do something for you to forgive."

"But why? Why would you make yourself so heavy, dark and
dense in order to do that?"

"Simple," the Friendly Soul said. "I would do it because I
love you."

The little soul seemed surprised at the answer.

"Don't be so amazed," said the Friendly Soul. "It's what we
all do for each other, just as God has said. So I will come and
be the 'bad one' for you. I will do something really terrible,
and then you can experience yourself as one who forgives."

"But what will you do," asked the little soul nervously, "that
will be so terrible?"

"Oh" replied the Friendly Soul with a twinkle, "We'll think
of something! But you are right about one thing, you know. I
will have to slow down my vibration and become very heavy
in order to do this not-so-nice thing. I will have to pretend to
be something very unlike myself. So I must ask one favor of
you in return."

"Oh, anything!" cried the little soul, who was now beginning
to dance and sing "I get to be forgiving, I get to be forgiving."

"Well," said the Friendly Soul, "In the moment that I strike you and smite you – in the moment that I do the worst to you that you could possibly imagine – in that very moment..."

"Yes?" interrupted the little soul.

"Remember who I am."

"Oh, I will!" cried the little soul, "I promise. I will always remember you as I see you right here, right now!"

"Good," said the Friendly Soul, "because, you see, I will have been pretending so hard, I will have forgotten myself. And if you don't remember me as I really am, I may not be able to remember for a very long time, and we will both be lost. Then we will need another soul to come along and remind us both who we are."

"No, we won't!" cried the little soul. "I will remember you! And I will thank you for bringing me this gift – the chance to experience myself as who I truly am."

And so the Agreement was made. And the little soul went forth into a new lifetime, excited to be the light –– especially that part called forgiveness. And the little soul waited anxiously to be able to experience itself as Forgiveness and to thank all the other souls that made it possible.

And at all the moments during its life, whenever a new soul appeared on the scene, whether that new soul brought joy or sadness – and especially if it brought sadness – the little soul thought of what God had said. "Always remember," God had smiled, "I have sent you nothing but angels."

Adapted from: **The Little Soul and the Sun,** *by Neale Donald Walsch. Published by Hampton Roads.*

Being willing to accept this world view requires a big shift in consciousness, and it is likely to take a lot of time and practice before victim consciousness begins to fade. It cannot be achieved without constant use of the Tipping Method tools.

And since we still operate in a world run by human law and rules of justice, we have to recognize that in the human reality there are indeed victims and perpetrators. At the same time, however, we need to hold in our minds that this is the illusion and that spiritual law is the only true law in universal terms.

25 Practical Uses for Radical Forgiveness:
Solving the Problems and Challenges of Everyday Life in a New Way

PART ONE

Applications for Better Health

1. Raise Your Vibration and Be Happy

2. Detox Your Body, Reduce Stress, Live Longer, and Enjoy Better Sex

3. Scrub Out Your Chakras and Heal from the Inside Out

4. Use the CancerHelp and Prevention Strategy

5. Lose Weight and Love Your Body

6. Control Perfectionism, Prevent CFS and Find Your Inner Slob

7. Overcome Your Addiction with RF as the Next Step

8. Release That Trauma and Let's Get On with Life

9. Manage Anger and Other Juicy Emotions

Application #1:

Raise Your Vibration and Be Happy

*Raising your vibration is the key to
wholeness, health and wealth.*

T houghts, beliefs, emotions, attitudes and behaviors all carry a certain vibrational frequency. The lower our vibratory rate the less healthy we are in mind, body and spirit.

David Hawkins, MD., Ph.D., in his groundbreaking book *Power vs. Force,* developed a scale of consciousness based on the vibratory rate of certain states of mind, those states being determined by the thoughts, attitudes and beliefs of the people who exist in that reality.

Quality	Log	Emotion
Peace	600	Bliss
Joy	540	Serenity
Love	500	Reverence
Reason	400	Understanding
Acceptance	350	Forgiveness
Willingness	310	Optimism
Neutrality	250	Trust
Courage	200	Affirmation
Pride	175	Scorn
Anger	150	Hate
Desire	125	Craving
Fear	100	Anxiety
Grief	75	Regret

Apathy	50	Despair
Guilt	30	Blame
Shame	20	Humiliation

David Hawkins, M.D., Ph.D. — Scale of Consciousness: *Power vs. Force.*

It is clear from the list that if your consciousness is dominated by fear, anger, resentment, pride, shame and guilt, you will carry a very low vibration. This will have a serious effect on every aspect of your life.

Like attracts like, so, through the law of resonance, you will tend to bring people to you with a similar vibration as well as circumstances of a similar vibration. It's simply how energy works. Anything below 200 is negative in the sense that someone or something vibrating below that mark is taking out of the system more energy than they are contributing.

Given the current mass consciousness, most people are vibrating below 200 most of the time because they are largely driven by fear, greed, competition, self-interest, pride, righteousness and prejudice, or in many parts of the world just pure survival.

Now, of course, for you and I that was OK while we were in the first phase of our soul's journey. We needed these kinds of energies to give us the experience we wanted, but now that we have awakened, we need to raise our vibration. One of the ways of doing that is to apply the Radical Forgiveness paradigm to all aspects of our lives which will automatically allow us to let go of toxic beliefs and attitudes not in alignment with the higher values associated with Radical Forgiveness.

Our goal is to get to the point where we vibrate fairly consistently between 350 - 400. This we can achieve by applying the philosophy of Radical Forgiveness to as many aspects of our lives as possible using the Applications provided in this series.

Of course, this does not mean that we will not feel angry, grief-stricken fearful or shameful at times. The point is to feel it and then move out of it as soon as possible. When we are angry, for example, we will be vibrating at around 150, which is not too bad actually, but it is not a place to hang out for long. Just doing a Radical Forgiveness worksheet will raise our vibration to around 350, according to Hawkins. If we follow it up a few days later with the 13 Steps Audio, we may raise it a notch or two higher, but more importantly, it will consolidate the upward shift in vibration.

Guilt and shame are more difficult because they have the lowest vibration of all. This makes it very hard to escape because look what is above them. Apathy. This is one reason why self-acceptance and self-forgiveness is experienced as almost impossible to achieve.

The more you use the Tipping Method Tools, the more grounded you will be in that higher vibration, the point being, of course, the higher your vibration the more powerful you become, the more healthy you become and the more peaceful you become. Furthermore, your contribution to the overall energy field of the planet and all life forms thereon will be a definite net positive.

According to Hawkins, while 85 percent of the population of the world calibrates well below the level of 200, it is the

33

counterbalancing power of the relatively few individuals near the top that brings the average to 207.

Hawkins' testing shows that one person vibrating at level 350 will counterbalance 190,000 individuals vibrating below 200. Someone at the level of 400 will counterbalance 400,000 people below 200, while someone vibrating at the level of 500 will counterbalance 750,000 individuals at less than 200. One individual at 600 counterbalances 10 million people under 200.

He says that after the critical shift at 200, the next critical change of consciousness happens at 350. At that level, individuals become aware that they are the source and creator of their life experience and develop the capacity to live harmoniously with the forces of life. That is to say, they have integrated and have begun to live Radical Forgiveness as their 'default' way of life.

If you were to reach 350-400, that would mean you would be able to hold the vibration of Radical Forgiveness virtually the whole time and nurture only thoughts of PEACE and LOVE, aware of the PERFECTION of what is occurring in your own life and out there in the world. It would also mean that you would, in effect, be counterbalancing approximately 200,000 people who might be in fear, anger, apathy and despair. Given that we have 237 million people in the U.S., it would only take around 2,000 people at the 350/400 level holding the vibration of PEACE to tip the scales in the direction of world peace. Isn't that exciting?

Anyway, at the more practical level, in order to raise our vibration and become more conscious, we need to submit all the old ideas, beliefs and prejudices we have held so strongly in the past about such things as race, gender, religion, politics and so on, to rigorous examination to see if they calibrate as having a high or low vibration.

To know the difference between the two, just notice how you feel in your body when you give them expression. If you really pay attention, you literally will feel your vibration go up or down in response to what you are saying or even thinking. As you practice this over time you will find yourself becoming more sensitive to the vibration of whatever is expressed.

While all those toxic beliefs and ideas served us well as instances of separateness and difference, they now serve only to block our energy flow and lower our vibration if we continue to hold onto them. They have to go.

For example, take the idea that women are inferior to men and should be treated as less than equal. In many places in the world, and in the majority of religions, this belief is still strong and women are seen as merely the property of men. This has been a perfect way for the human group soul, as well as individual souls, to feel the pain of separation, but it is inherently an idea which carries a very low vibration. Once we have awakened, it needs to be purged from our consciousness. Rooted in the male ego, not only does it fly in the face of the spiritual truth that we are One, but the idea is immoral, inhuman and indefensible. How could it possibly raise one's vibration? It is an idea that is inherently toxic.

This is a good one to practice releasing from your consciousness, if only because it is so ingrained in you. It's in every one of us, women included. It operates below the level of awareness

35

most of the time, of course, but if you are willing to take this idea into meditation for a while, look at it and own it, even for just a moment, you will feel its vibration. You will feel yours go down. If you then make a conscious decision to adopt a thought that women and men are equal and you intend to treat both with love and respect, you will feel your vibration become higher and you will feel better.

On a practical level, any time you become aware of anyone acting out or expressing this or any other low vibration idea, you should do a Radical Forgiveness worksheet on that person, especially if what you see or hear upsets you emotionally. It means that person is a mirror for you, offering you the opportunity to love the part of yourself that is being reflected.

As you forgive that person, you heal that part of you. And as we have seen, whenever you do this, not only does it help you to raise your own vibration and increases your happiness, it contributes to an overall raising of the vibration of the planet. This idea is developed fully in Applications 24 and 25.

Another set of toxic thoughts, judgments and beliefs that need to be released are those you have created about yourself. Just as the human group soul has created separation between male and female, so we have created separation within ourselves. But we shall leave this for deeper treatment in Application 15.

RESOURCES FOR THIS APPLICATION: (Details in Resources Section at the back of this book and at www.radicalforgiveness.com.)

Worksheet: Radical Forgiveness Worksheet

Application #2:

Detox Your Body, Reduce Stress, Live Longer, and Enjoy Better Sex

*If we used Radical Forgiveness to regularly dissolve
mental, emotional and spiritual toxicity,
I believe we would never get sick.*

Radical Forgiveness has proven to be a powerful modality for healing and for the promotion of health in mind, body and spirit. It has earned the right to claim to be a powerful detoxification mechanism, an efficient stress management system and a guaranteed way to conserve life-force energy.

Given that it exhibits these life-enhancing attributes, it is quite reasonable to expect the regular use of Radical Forgiveness to increase life expectancy. And although we cannot guarantee better sex, if it's all about energy why would we not expect that to be improved as well? Bear in mind, too, that Radical Forgiveness works wonders for relationships, so it definitely is a possibility!

Not so long ago, health was defined as the absence of disease. As we have become more knowledgeable about how our bodies really work, we have begun to define it differently. We now see optimum health in terms of how well our life-force energy flows through our body and the level at which we vibrate energetically. It is now well understood that we become sick when our energy gets stuck and our vibration goes down and stays down.

37

This happens whenever we judge, make someone wrong, blame, project our pain onto others, repress anger, hold resentment, and all other forms of mental, emotional and spiritual toxicity. In other words it occurs when we play life according to the rules of victim consciousness.

The relatively new science of psychoneuroimmunology has laid the scientific foundation for a medical model that recognizes and takes account of the essential interplay between mind, body and spirit in the creation of health. These scientists are proving that, for optimum health, our life-force energy must be able to flow freely through the mind/body/ spirit system. If our filters become clogged with mental, emotional and spiritual toxicity, our life force stops flowing freely, our vibration is lowered and our body starts shutting down. Eventually, our body gets sick, and, if the toxic blocks are not removed, we may die, or, at best, live a less than healthy life.

I learned recently that in the UK, one in four people have been prescribed anti-depressants at some time in their lives.[1] In America, the use of anti-depressants skyrocketed by 400% in two decades.[2]

Of course, there are people who are really suffering with clinical depression and for whom such medications are a godsend. But I'm sure that is a tiny minority out of all those taking these drugs. Most are taking them to mask the pain caused by the toxic energy that is clogging their minds, their hearts and their spirit. They are taking them because they know no other way to dull the pain. Others resort to alcohol for the same reason while millions of people are prescribed drugs like Valium to reduce their anxiety.

I am convinced that if they would only use Radical Forgiveness to detoxify their minds, bodies and souls, they would have no need for chemical interventions.

While the medical profession has been slow to accept the idea that mental and emotional factors play a huge part in causing disease and malfunction in the physical body, they all now recognize that stress is a killer. When people go for their annual check-ups, I doubt there are many doctors who fail to entreat them to reduce their stress levels. That's especially true if the person already is showing symptoms of heart disease, which we all know is the biggest killer today. Stress kills. And it often kills early.

There are many forms of stress, but the kind of emotional stress that comes with the feeling of having been seriously victimized is an extremely potent form of stress that, if not released, is long-lasting, debilitating and potentially lethal. There is no doubt whatsoever that it causes many diseases, including cancer. (See Application #4 for more on this.)

Radical Forgiveness reframes past events where you felt you were victimized, detoxifying all the stress-inducing ideas, thoughts and beliefs you may be obsessing about. If you use it in your everyday life, it will prevent the buildup of toxicity that would otherwise create disease. It will keep your vibration high and your filters clean.

That's the gift of Radical Forgiveness, and that's why it qualifies as a potent form of preventive medicine. If we used it all the time to deal with mental, emotional and spiritual toxicity as it occurs, I believe we would seldom get sick.

I don't think I need to belabor the point. You know your own body and you probably know what stresses you out and makes you feel bad. Re-read Chapter 2 on victim consciousness again, and bring to mind all your victim stories. Start making your forgiveness list. By the time you have read this book, you will have quite a list, I'm sure. And a lot of forgiveness work to do. But it will be worth it. Your health depends on it.

In the next application, you will discover a way to find out whose energy you have stuck in which of your chakras, and how that might be affecting your health.

RESOURCES FOR THIS APPLICATION: (Details in Resources Section at the back of this book and at www.radicalforgiveness.com.)

Worksheet: The Radical Forgiveness Worksheet

Audio: The 3-Part Set: Radical Forgiveness

Audio: The Radical Forgiveness Meditations

Application #3:

Scrub Out Your Chakras and Heal From the Inside Out

*Having your chakras balanced and your Etheric Body
cleansed will allow your life energy to flow naturally,
inviting your body's natural healing process
to heal your body, mind, and spirit
from the inside out*

In the previous chapter, I advanced the idea that optimum health is a question of how freely one's life-force energy flows through our physical body. Anything that causes a restriction in that flow is likely to eventually create some kind of symptom of disease or illness occurring in the body. We know that negative beliefs, thoughts, attitudes, traumas, emotional wounds, secrets, addictions or any kind of victim story, can block the energy flow and cause real physical problems.

Biologist Bruce Lipton has shown that each individual cell is physically affected and changed by the energies attached to these things. This gives credence to the idea that our victim stories live in our bodies at the cellular level. To employ computer language for a moment, to maintain our health we need to 'uninstall' the old victim story program and 'install' the new one. We do that using the Radical Forgiveness technology.

But we are more than just a physical body. We have five bodies in total, all of which are involved in the healing process. Each one is more subtle than the next and one octave higher in vibration.

They are: 1. The Physical Body; 2. The Etheric Body; 3. The Emotional Body.; 4. The Mental Body and 5. The Spiritual Body

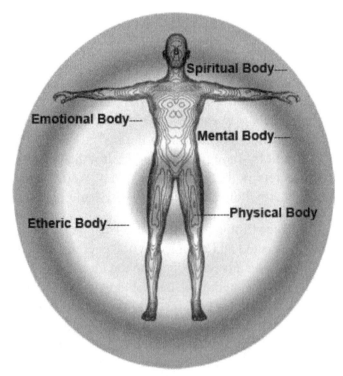

Fig. 4: *The Five Bodies*

The physical body is vibrationally the most dense and is the one that vibrates at the level at which it becomes physical form. The others are not normally visible to most people, though some are able to register them as an aura around the physical body.

Physical healing requires change at the cellular level so our bodies become clear of toxic energy. But with Radical Forgiveness, we apparently work not with the physical body, but with the body's energetic blueprint, which is held in the Etheric Body.

The blueprint is the energetic template for the physical body and is responsible for it always remaining the same even though the body is constantly dying and being reborn every moment. The blueprint accesses your genetic code and holds the memory of who you are, the shape of your nose, your height, what you like to eat, your strength, your weakness, your illness patterns, and so forth. It has a direct relationship to how well the physical body functions.

Some parts of our body replicate themselves very quickly. The liver, for example, renews itself every 14 days. In one year, our whole body has done the same thing. I do not occupy the same body I did a year ago. I look and operate pretty much the same only because the Etheric Body has the blueprint and is in charge of the entire makeover.

When we carry mental, emotional and spiritual toxicity in those respective subtle bodies, it eventually filters down into the blueprint. Then, as Bruce Lipton has shown, it ends up in our cells.

From then on, unless that blueprint is modified, those cells containing all that toxicity get replicated just like any other cell. The Etheric Body is altogether neutral in this regard. It just does what it is supposed to do, which is replicate, replicate, replicate.

Our wounds may well begin in the spiritual body and be processed within the mental and emotional bodies; but they crystalize in the etheric, specifically in one or more of the seven chakras located in the Etheric Body, as energetic patterns within the overall blueprint that will, if not dispersed, determine your life and your health. We can heal ourselves in mind, body and spirit, from the inside out, by working with these chakras.

Chakras are not physical in nature, but they are connected to certain glands and organs within the physical body. The Chakras act like transformers. They take in and utilize the energy or life force, sometimes known as prana, chi or Christ energy, which comes to us from the universe. They step this energy down to frequencies that can be used by the bio-molecular and cellular processes of the physical body.

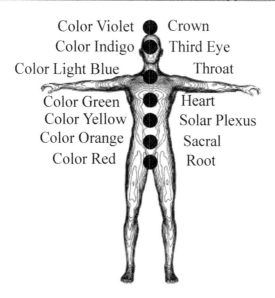

Color Violet — Crown
Color Indigo — Third Eye
Color Light Blue — Throat
Color Green — Heart
Color Yellow — Solar Plexus
Color Orange — Sacral
Color Red — Root

Fig. 5: The Seven Chakras

The chakras also represent the locations where each of the subtle bodies link to the physical body, thus bringing different levels of consciousness into our being. They process our daily experiences, thoughts and feelings, while also carrying long-term data relating to personal and tribal history, long-established thought patterns and archetypes.

The first three chakras, the root, sacral and solar plexus, possess levels of consciousness that vibrate at the lower frequencies of the existential chain and remain rooted in the World of Humanity. The consciousness that comes through the fifth (the throat), sixth (the third eye), and seventh (the crown) are more likely to align with the energies from the World of Spirit.

The fourth, the heart chakra, provides the link between the World of Humanity and the World of Divine Truth. The heart is the center of our being.

The chakras are crucial to our health, spiritual well-being and vibratory rate. When the chakras become out of balance – as they do when we become emotionally upset or traumatized for instance – they reverse rotation, become very erratic and, in some cases, close down almost entirely.

Anger, resentment and hurt will tend to close the heart and throat chakras. Guilt and lack of trust will weaken the sacral chakra, and so on. The effects of such energy imbalances will be felt as lethargy, a general malaise, low sex drive, inability to speak our truth and symptoms for which a medical cause cannot be found.

Having your chakras balanced and etheric body cleansed is important. This will allow your life-force energy to flow naturally, allowing your body's natural healing process to heal your body, mind, and spirit.

Drawing on the work of Caroline Myss, the author of *The Anatomy of Spirit,* we can take this further by identifying which of the many non-forgiveness issues are likely to be held in each of the chakras. This then reveals whose energy you are holding in your own etheric field and, consequently, who it is you need to forgive.

Unless you are willing to go to quite some effort and preparation, a chakra balance and etheric cleansing needs to be done with a practitioner, since it involves the use of stones, oils and a pendulum. But if you are willing to do the research and wish to do it all yourself, here's how you do it:

Find out which of several stones and types of essential oils are associated with each chakra. After holding the stone in your hand over the relevant chakra for a few seconds, use a pendulum to ask if the chakra is in or out of balance. *(You need to know how your pendulum indicates Yes and No before you ask the question.)* If it is out of balance, take a strong sniff of the oil and then check again. This should be enough to bring that chakra back into balance. If not, take another sniff and check again. Then do it again, but this time speak out loud the person's name you may still have an issue with. Check your chakra again to see if it is balanced. If it is, say the following four statements from the Emerge-n-see 4-Step process in your mind:

1. Look what I created.
2. I notice my judgments and feeling but love myself anyway.
3. I am willing to see the perfection in the situation and realize there is nothing to forgive.
4. I choose peace.

Then check again, and if necessary sniff that oil again. Hopefully you will be in balance.

Shari Claire, one of our Senior Radical Forgiveness Coaches with the Institute for Radical Forgiveness, has created a special Etheric Cleansing and Chakra Balancing meditation that makes it possible for you to go through the process on your own, simply by listening to the recording and participating as instructed.

She suggested I record the meditation, so it is my voice on the CD. It also tells you exactly how to obtain stones and oils specific to each chakra and pendulums.

This meditation will assist you in detoxing the chakras/energy centers of your body, and at the same time cleanse all five of your subtle bodies.

Who's That In My Chakra Making Me Sick?
You can use what we learned here to find out who you need to forgive in order to be healthy in mind, body and spirit. If you already have developed symptoms in a particular area of your body connected to a particular chakra, this might show you who you need to forgive and for what. Even if you have no symptoms there now, it could be showing you who to forgive, as a preventive measure.

I recommend you do the following experiment before reading any further. This will show you where in your body and in which chakra you might have some toxic energy to clear.

Exercise:
1. Make a list of all the people you feel have done something to you to upset you and/or make you feel like a victim, from now all the way back to childhood. Include yourself if you want. The people can be alive or dead. They can be people you know, or people like politicians or officials you don't personally know but who have done you 'wrong' in some way. God might be in there, too. Parents are almost certain to make the list.

2. Put each name on the smallest 'Post-it®' you have and put to one side.

3. Take 7 sheets of paper, A4 or Letter size. On the top of the first one, put a red blob, fairly large and strongly colored. Use markers if you have them. Then on the next one, do an orange blob, then yellow on the next one, then green, then sky blue, then indigo blue and then violet. Then lay all seven sheets out on the floor or put them up on the wall.

4. The next step has to be entirely intuitive. No thinking allowed. Just do what your gut tells you to do. You take each 'Post-it®,' look at the name for a couple of seconds, and stick it on the sheet you feel led to put it on. Do not think about it or pay any thoughtful attention to the color on the top of the sheet of paper.

5. In her book, *Anatomy of Spirit*, Caroline Myss indicates how each of the seven main chakras hold the energy attached to an issue, or groups of issues. Myss specifies the following generalized issues associated with each chakra, and indicates the areas of the body affected. Look at the names you have put next to a particular color on one sheet and ask yourself:

a) Do those things Myss identifies with this color apply to the people I have put on the sheet displaying that same color?

b) Do I have any symptoms in my body that correspond to the areas Myss identifies as being associated with this chakra?

49

CROWN: Color: Violet.
People with these characteristics or traits may resonate for you issues such as: Trust in life itself. Values, ethics, courage, humanitarianism, selflessness, faith and inspiration, and your ability to see the big picture.
Affecting: Skin, bones, muscles.

3RD EYE: Color: Indigo.
People with these characteristics or traits may resonate for you issues connected to: Truth, awareness, self-awareness, intuition, knowledge, and ability to learn from experience. Emotional intelligence. Psychic ability.
Affecting: Brain, nerves, eyes, ears, nose, pineal, pituitary.

THROAT: Color: Sky Blue.
People with these characteristics or traits may resonate for you issues connected to: Strength of will, personal expression and communication, following your dream or using your personal power to create or make decisions. Addiction, judgment & criticism.
Affecting: Thyroid, neck, mouth, parathyroid, hypothalamus.

HEART: Color: Green.
People with these characteristics or traits may resonate for you issues connected to: Love & hatred. Resentment and bitterness. Grief and anger. Self-centeredness, loneliness, commitment, forgiveness, compassion. Hope & trust.
Affecting: All chest area & thymus gland.

SOLAR PLEXUS: Color: Yellow.
People with these characteristics or traits may resonate for you issues connected to: Intimidation,

personal power, confidence and honor. Distrust of others and low self-esteem. Co-dependency, sensitivity to criticism and ability to take care of oneself.
Affecting: Stomach, liver, gall bladder, pancreas, adrenals, spleen, mid-spine.

SACRAL: Color: Orange.
People with these characteristics or traits may resonate for you issues connected to: Money, sex, creativity and relationships. Blame and guilt. Ethics and honor in relationships.
Affecting: Genitals, pelvis, low back, appendix, hips, bladder.

ROOT: Color: Red.
People with these characteristics or traits may resonate for you issues connected to: Tribal Energy. Family and group safety or lack thereof. Feeling at home or not accepted, basic security or lack of it. (Ability to stand up for yourself and to provide for yourself. Social and family law and order.)
Affecting: Body support, coccyx, sacrum, feet, rectum, prostate, immune system.

How you answer questions (a) and (b) will tell you who you need to forgive and in what order of priority. If you already have symptoms in the area in question and you have identified someone there, you need to focus on forgiving that person first and then look to see if that makes any difference to your symptomology. But don't ignore the others. By doing the forgiveness work on them, you may be preventing something that might be on its way in.

In about a week's time, do the exercise again to see if you might put someone in a different chakra. It is not unusual for a person, especially a parent, to show up in more than one chakra. So it's not wrong. In fact it is giving you more detailed information.

For example, suppose someone turns up in red one week and blue the next. Well, that could mean he or she is making you feel unsafe by what he/she is saying or not saying. Another example is if someone shows up in the yellow one week and orange the next. You then look at the possibility that the person is or was trying to control you through money or sex. You just put the two together.

RESOURCES FOR THIS APPLICATION: (Details in Resources Section at the back of this book and at www.radicalforgiveness.com.)

Worksheet: Radical Forgiveness Worksheet

Audio: Radical Forgiveness Chakra Meditation & Etheric Cleansing Meditation

---

Application #4:

A CancerHelp and Prevention Strategy

People who develop a strategy of dealing with their emotions by burying them, rather than feeling them, are statistically more likely to get cancer than those who are willing to feel their feelings and process them as and when they arise.

In the previous applications we covered, in general terms at least, how Radical Forgiveness can make a significant impact on our level of physical health. I do feel, however, that cancer prevention through Radical Forgiveness deserves its own place.

This is because there is a significant amount of respectable research directed towards establishing proof that there is a definite causal link between cancer and emotional stress. (For emotional stress, read "unresolved emotional traumas," repressed emotions like grief, anger, sorrow and so on, the very things that Radical Forgiveness is so good at releasing.)

We also emphasized in Application #2 the role of toxic beliefs in creating the conditions in which disease can enter the body. Here is one I purposely left out in order to give it to you in this chapter.

In his classic book, *Cancer as a Turning Point,* published in 1989, psychotherapist Lawrence LeShan outlined his finding, researched over many years of working with cancer patients, that virtually all of them had the same core-negative belief:

"If I show up as who I am, I will not be loved. Therefore to be loved, I must pretend to be who I am not."

How about that for a toxic belief? From that we might conclude that cancer has its roots in self-hatred, and then is fed by the rage the person with cancer has towards the people who made them feel they were not okay the way they were. Who else could that be but their parents? It was probably completely unintended, of course, and it was what their Higher Self chose, as we now know.

If you have a belief that is anywhere close to that one and you don't want to become another statistic, now is the time to do the Radical Forgiveness work on your parents as well as some Self-Acceptance work on yourself. This will be especially important to you if cancer is in your family, which brings me to another point.

There is agreement amongst the scientists that, while there are many factors that can be causal in nature, there are only two conditions that are actually statistically accurate predictors of who will get the disease. The first is having the cancer gene. The second is if you suppress or repress strong emotions.

The genetic factor is quite well publicized, most recently by the movie star Angelina Jolie, who, having seen how prevalent breast cancer was in her family, chose to have a double mastectomy as a preventive measure.

Less well-publicized, but nevertheless well-proven in a study by British scientist Steven Greer[1], is the fact that people who develop a strategy of dealing with their emotions by burying them rather than feeling them are statistically more likely to get cancer than those who are willing to feel their feelings and process them as and when they arise.

It may have been prudent in a case such as Angelina's to take that course of action, but for someone who has cancer or is pre-cancerous but lacking the strong genetic link, it would be equally prudent to look for a causal link that is emotional in nature. For example, when I meet someone with breast cancer, I ask always ask, "Who broke your heart around 5 or 7 years prior to the onset of the cancer?" They can usually come up with a name immediately. Using the knowledge about what issues tend to be in what chakra and in what part of the body, one could ask a similar question about any cancer located there.

This puts Radical Forgiveness front and center as the main prevention measure in this case. It's a no-brainer, isn't it? The way to do it is to go back over your life and systematically clean that energy out of your body using the simple tools we supply. It's not hard and costs next to nothing.

The Cancer Personality
To give you more information to assess your own risk of getting cancer, people who use this strategy of stoically denying their feelings are people who conform to what has come to be known as the Type C personality. This is virtually the same as 'the cancer personality,' described by the well-known scientist and cancer researcher O. Carl Simonton.[2]

It is descriptive of someone who tends to repress their emotions, maintains a facade of pleasantness, never expresses anger and strives excessively to please authority figures.

They are self-sacrificing, unassertive people who focus their attention on others and away from themselves. They are the classic co-dependents.

When my wife JoAnn and I were running CancerHelp retreats in the North Georgia Mountains called *The Georgia CancerHelp Program,* I would spend hours on the phone talking with people who said they really wanted to come, but could not do so because it might put someone out. One woman said, "I would really love to come to the retreat but my son said he was coming over to see me that weekend and he would be so upset if I was not there." My response? "Well then, keep your cancer. That's why you have it. You make others more important than yourself – your own healing, no less." It made no impression on her. She just said, "Well, he's such a good boy."

People tend to think of Type 'C' individuals as nice people, very caring and generous. Outwardly, they are. On the inside, though, they are full of repressed rage and resentment. They are not aware of it, of course, but since depression is a symptom of repressed rage, you will find that many Type Cs are on anti-depressants.

Again, is this you? If so, according to clinical psychologist Lydia Temoshok (*The Type C Connection*) and science writer Henry Dreher (*Your Defense Against Cancer*), you would be more vulnerable to cancer than people who are more assertive and self-serving. This is not meant to scare you but to give you an opportunity to take some preventive action with Radical Forgiveness to reduce the risk.

There's no need to labor the point. I'm sure it is quite clear to you now that Radical Forgiveness is a really good process for preventing cancer, or at least reducing the risk.

If you already have a diagnosis of cancer, I am convinced that Radical Forgiveness should be a significant part of whatever protocol you are using to treat the disease. Most oncologists these days are well aware of the influence of emotions and will support you in doing this work in addition to whatever course of treatment you wish to pursue. If you get someone who does not support it, I would suggest you look for someone who does.

Preventing a Recurrence
I see a lot of people who receive treatment, are pronounced cancer free, and go right back to business as usual. Same diet, same stress levels, no change. They are kidding themselves that they are 'cured.' and can just go on as before.

I believe that cancer is a message that change is required. In that sense it is a loving message. In the CancerHelp retreats that my wife and I ran, our aim was to have them loving and appreciating their cancer by the end of 5 days because of the gifts that came from it. It was not unusual for them to say, "Cancer was the best thing that ever happened to me." It changed their lives.

We have to remember, there is no definite cure for cancer. It can come back and frequently does. A cure is considered to be no recurrence within 5 years. Nevertheless, there is still an unspoken expectation that a recurrence is almost inevitable and just a question of time. If repressed emotions and unresolved victim stories were implicated in causing the cancer in the first place, and they have not been released during the first round of treatment or soon after, I would agree. It is highly likely it will return because the toxic cause has not been dealt with. Need I say more?

RESOURCES FOR THIS APPLICATION: (Details in Resources Section at the back of this book and at www.radicalforgiveness.com.)

Book: *Radical Forgiveness*

Worksheet: Radical Forgiveness Worksheet.

DVD: Cancer and Radical Forgiveness

Application #5:

Lose Weight and Love Your Body

"The Only Things You Have to Give Up Are the Stories That Caused the Weight Gain in the First Place."

In this application we take a look at how Radical Forgiveness can help with the issue of weight and body image. Very few people say they are really happy with their bodies. In fact, I would say that for many of us, our bodies are a great source of shame and even self-hatred. Let's see if we can understand why.

[Note: I wish to disclose here that at certain points in this application, I am drawing verbatim on some of what I have written in the chapter on weight issues in my book, *Radical Manifestation: The Fine Art of Creating the Life You Want.*]

One thing that psychology teaches us is that we all have a large measure of self-hatred in our unconscious minds. Carl Jung referred to this as our shadow – everything about ourselves that we are ashamed of or feel guilty about that we have pushed down deep, well out of our awareness. That way we never have to look at it again, much less deal with.

Much of it is gained during our early years, but we also carry a great deal of collective guilt and shame from past generations – even in our DNA. It is locked away somewhere deep down, and heaven help anything that causes it to come up or even begin to come into our conscious awareness.

59

Fortunately, or unfortunately, depending on your point of view, there is a way to stop it from coming into our awareness - it's called projection.

Fig. 6: *Projection*

One way in which we use projection is to find someone who exhibits that very same quality we hate in ourselves, and then hurl our self-hatred onto them. We make them our scapegoats. We criticize them, even demonize them in order to make sure that the self-hatred remains 'out there' rather than 'in here.' We have no idea that we are doing it, of course.

Another type of projection is to push our self-hatred onto our bodies. This is very common. We make our bodies our scapegoats. We pour hatred into our bodies and treat them badly. In this we are aided by the way society in general and the advertising industry in particular promotes the idea that there is such a thing as the ideal body to which we should all aspire.

60

Actually, when you think about it, it's quite amazing how much importance we attach to the body and the degree to which we identify with it. We focus an enormous amount of attention upon it. Given the size and economic importance of the fashion industry, you could even say we are obsessed with it. No wonder we become convinced that we are our bodies!

The truth is, of course, that we are not our bodies. We existed before we had a body, and we will continue to exist after we have experienced our physical death and dropped the body. Just like we rent a car for a specific journey, the body is something we take on and use for the duration of this leg of our Soul's journey, and then discard once the journey is over.

Why Take on a Body?
In spite of our obsession with the physical body, and as much as we have studied it and come to know its intricate workings, we have all but ignored the most fundamental question of all: Why do we have a body? Why would a spiritual being, who is free to move around at will within the World of Divine Existence, decide to lower its vibration and become encumbered with a body that is dense, heavy and prone to breaking down on a regular basis?

As I have explained earlier, I believe the reason we do it is to be able to experience separation and all that comes with it. We do it in order to develop a deeper awareness of 'Oneness.'

The first order of separation is to experience ourselves as individuals, each with our own bodies. Another part of our agreement with Spirit, according to the Radical Forgiveness story, is to have the experience of separation as an emotional event. And for that, a body is essential. Without a body, you cannot feel. So the primary function of the body is to give us the opportunity to feel our feelings and to have emotions.

Body Hatred

If the body is our spiritual vehicle for taking us into and through the deep pain of separation, is it any wonder that we are not only obsessed with our bodies, but essentially hate them for precisely that reason? Even though our memories of existence prior to incarnation are dim at best, or for the most part non-existent, don't you think that part of us might remember what it is like to be just spirit and not encumbered with a body?

Isn't it possible that we might have some resentment about having to carry this burden? If so, doesn't it make sense that we might project all our guilt and rage about being separate and in pain onto our body? After all, having taken on a body as a symbol of separation, it follows that the body must also symbolize the intense pain that inevitably accompanies the sense of separation.

The Weight Issue

The one body issue over which we constantly obsess is the issue of weight. It serves as one of the most convenient targets for our self-hatred. The weight loss industry is enormously profitable. It is kept running by how society in general and the media in particular aggressively promote the notion of the ideal body, the criteria for which very few people can ever even hope to meet.

But many aspire to it nevertheless, doing crazy things in order to get close to it at least, including endless diets, fasts, exercise programs, etc. None work for the vast majority of people, leading only to more self-hatred. It is a vicious circle, and if excessive weight gain was indeed invented by Spirit to provide an endless stream of painful separation in the form of self-rejection, then I guess it has been very successful. But from a human perspective, it is the source of a great deal of shame. That shame morphs into a whole series of negative "I AM" beliefs, like "I *am* worthless," "I *am* unlovable," "I *am* no good," and so on.

Millions of dollars each year are spent by hundreds of thousands of people trying to lose weight through dieting, exercise, drugs, supplements, hypnosis and other weight control measures. Most of them fail, especially in the long term. They may produce a short-term weight loss, but invariably it comes back on.

The vast majority of programs focus on the physical factors associated with excessive weight gain. They virtually ignore or, at best, give only a passing nod to the emotional factors. My intention in this section, therefore, is to address head-on some of the emotional issues that seem to explain why people pack on the weight and adopt life-style patterns that only add to the problem.

Physical and Emotional
In my experience helping people deal with their emotional issues through Radical Forgiveness, I have noticed that these emotional issues are frequently reflected in their physical body in some way or another. It can appear as disease, tissue breakdown, immune system failure and so on, but for a great many people, it is reflected in the form of excess weight.

The ratio between physical and emotional factors in accounting for weight gain is difficult to calculate, but I would hazard a guess that most people's weight problems are somewhere in the region of 75 percent physical and lifestyle-related in nature and 25 percent emotional. This will obviously vary from person to person. In my workshops especially, I have encountered people I would have thought had that ratio reversed. Even then this is a false distinction since many of the physical factors themselves have an emotional cause or, at the very least, an emotional component.

As we saw in previous applications, our bodies reflect our emotional health. Some deal with their emotions by suppressing and repressing their feelings, which is an extremely unhealthy strategy. Repressed emotional baggage can manifest as disease, or it can literally show up as physical baggage in the form of excess weight, thereby serving the function of smothering the pain.

No amount of dieting will get rid of excess body fat if it is serving an emotional function. The most common function it performs is protection. This can be protection from generalized hurt and rejection, but most frequently it is used to protect from imagined or real sexual attack.

Protection
This is not just applicable to a small number of people. The sexual abuse of children by their parents, grandparents, step-parents, mothers' boyfriends, siblings, baby-sitters and others is rampant in our society. It is estimated that one in five adults was sexually molested in their childhood years.

The only way a powerless child can deal with such a severe wounding is through the mental mechanisms of denial, repression and disassociation. However, such attacks leave a powerful energetic imprint on the body, generated and sustained by a potent mixture of unresolved fear and guilt. The guilt arises because they nearly always think of it as their fault, frequently made worse by their own mother's refusing to believe them, if and when they have summoned enough courage to tell. The result is that they simply end up being blamed and punished even more.

The Body Remembers
Even if the mind blocks it out, the cellular structure of the body remembers only too well. So it seeks to protect itself by piling on the fat in those regions previously most affected and thought to be most vulnerable. This not only provides a wall of physical protection against attack, but psychic protection also.

The mind reasons that being physically attractive is a risky proposition, so the best way to ward off physical advances is by making oneself decidedly unattractive. What better way to become sexually unattractive than to be obese?

Self-Hatred
The body can also put on excess weight as a way to reinforce feelings of inadequacy and being unloved. It is a self-fulfilling prophecy that feeds on itself. The worse I feel about myself, the fatter I become. The fatter I become, the worse I feel about myself. And so it goes, on and on.

It is difficult to know for sure, but I would be willing to hazard a guess that well over half of those who are grossly

65

overweight are that way because they have deeply buried unconscious emotional pain that they are either not aware of or won't deal with.

The Solution

The obvious answer is Radical Forgiveness. It is the technology that hundreds of victims of sexual and other forms of abuse have used to neutralize and dissolve the energy patterns keeping the guilt, shame and fear frozen in their bodies and surrounded by fat.

The big advantage of the Radical Forgiveness approach is that it does not require the person to remember what happened, or go through the pain of re-enacting the experience. The Radical Forgiveness process is enough.

It is not uncommon for therapists, especially those who are abuse 'survivors' themselves, to strongly suggest that their clients confront their abusers and accuse them of their crime. I have yet to see this result in any kind of a healing. It invariably causes a dramatic worsening of the relationship and an increase in the pain for both parties. With Radical Forgiveness, the confrontation is not necessary. In fact, it is always counterproductive; it is much better that the work be done energetically and within your own mind.

The pain that the person feels is in direct proportion to the emotional energy invested, not so much in the event itself, but in the "story" of what happened. That story is composed of all the thoughts, assumptions, beliefs, feelings, memories and fears connected to the abuse. Most of it is repressed and therefore unconscious. That's not to say the pain isn't real, but what is clear is that the emotional energy invested in the story accounts for a disproportionate amount of the suffering. (Pain is what we experience in direct response to an event. Suffering comes as a result of the thoughts and beliefs we create about the event.)

For example, people who have experienced abuse typically have formed such self-deprecating, wounding beliefs as, *"I am damaged goods; I am no good; I don't deserve respect; I don't count; my needs don't matter; I am flawed; I am dirty; I can't say no; I will never be appreciated for who I am; men will always abuse me,"* and so on. This is what creates the suffering.

The emotional energy invested eventually crystallizes into a highly integrated energy field located in the body. It is this energy field which holds the story in place and keeps the suffering going on.

The way to heal the pain and suffering, therefore, is to simply dissolve that energy field using the tools of Radical Forgiveness. Once the energy field has collapsed, the story itself loses its power and begins to fade away. There is absolutely no need to go digging up the past, reliving the experience or confronting the abuser.

The dissolution of the energy field occurs through the Radical Forgiveness process, which comprises the following five stages. I outlined them earlier, but I would like to expand on them.

1. Telling the Abuse Victim Story
Here the person tells the story as he or she knows it

consciously. There is no need to try dredging up the unconscious stuff through hypnosis, nor even to prove that it happened. It doesn't matter whether it is true or false, since the objective is not to confront anyone with it.

[If legal proceedings are necessary, that is a separate issue. Nothing I say here has anything to do with what the law might say about the abuse, or what need there may be to protect others from the abuser.]

2. Feeling the Feelings

This usually happens as a consequence of telling the story and is an essential part of the process. It is also the part that most people try to avoid. The common ways to avoid it are to intellectualize it, trivialize it, or "spiritualize" it. We call the latter doing a "spiritual bypass." It is only through accessing and being willing to fully express the feelings we have attached to the situation that the process of dissolving the energy field can begin.

3. Collapsing the Energy Field

The energy field begins to collapse when, having expressed our rage, grief, sadness and hurt, we open our minds and hearts to all the factors relevant to the situation. When we begin to distinguish what in the story is fact and what is interpretation, we begin to see what really matters, what is meaningless and what needs are being served by holding onto the story. This is partly rational analysis, but in the context of Radical Forgiveness, it is just one step in the process of dissolving the energy field and NOT a complete "therapy" in and of itself. We also bring some understanding and compassion to the situation, allowing ourselves to be in the other person's shoes in order to understand why they did what they did. For example, in most cases, the abuser was also abused as a child and was acting out his or her pain. Knowing things like that helps. But it is still not Radical Forgiveness.

4. Reframing the Story

This is the Radical Forgiveness step. It occurs when we open up to the possibility that, if we could see the spiritual big picture (which we cannot), we would become aware that what happened was part of a Divine plan and was intended for our soul's growth. Therefore in that sense nothing wrong happened.

Now, as we know, that is a very difficult idea to accept, and right now the only way we can even work with it is to use a Radical Forgiveness worksheet that enables us to say "Yes" to it, even when we don't believe it. As we have said before, *willingness* to entertain the possibility that there is perfection in the situation is sufficient for it to work.

5. Integrate the Story

This involves doing something physical to complete the energetic exchange and to replace, in the physical body at the cellular level, the victim story with the new "perfection" story. This is accomplished by doing the worksheet or using one or more of the other tools. One of the most powerful ways to integrate is to do a supervised session of breathwork.

Doing the Radical Forgiveness process does more than make the person doing the forgiving feel better. Not only does it collapse the energy field attached to his or her own personal story, but it begins to collapse the entire energy field surrounding the abuse situation itself, as well as all those involved, including the abuser.

Because they all belong to the same "morphogenetic field,"* everyone feels it, and everyone has free will to respond to it in whatever way is best for them spiritually.

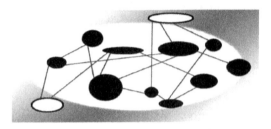

Fig. 7: *A Morphogenetic Field*

[*A morphogenetic field and morphic resonance are terms coined by biologist, Rupert Sheldrake, author of A New Science of Life, 1995, to explain how information is transferred energetically between people irrespective of distance.]

However, all the people involved, other than the one forgiving, have no conscious awareness of any change occurring because it all occurs at the energetic level. Yet they might begin to feel differently and perhaps spontaneously do something, like communicate or take some action that might lead to a genuine healing of some sort. Our experience is that this kind of thing is not uncommon and is likely to happen when there has been no confrontation.

It also resolves the issue of whether the abuse actually happened. Many people have what we call flashbacks or spontaneous recall of early childhood abuse events. This gives those who don't want to believe that the abuse happened to the person an opportunity to cast doubt on the claim. They might say that the therapist with unresolved abuse issues might have been unconsciously transferring his or her energy to the client, or that it might have been a past-life recall or bleed through from the collective unconscious.

However, when we deal with it through Radical Forgiveness, none of this matters. Whatever the origin of the energy field, it is dissolved. The person is free to get on with his or her life, no one is accused, falsely or otherwise, and the likelihood of relationships becoming healed is really quite good. Everyone wins with a weight loss program based on Radical Forgiveness. It will help you:

1. Discover why the fat is there and what story supports it.
2. Recognize your body's need to hold onto it.
3. Forgive whoever created your need to hold the weight.
4. Let go of the weight now no longer serving a purpose.
5. Love yourself and your new body.

71

RESOURCES FOR THIS APPLICATION:
(Details in Resources Section at the back of this book and at www.radicalforgiveness.com.)

Book: *Radical Manifestation, The Fine Art of Creating the Life You Want.*

Online Program: *Radical Weight Loss Program.*

Application #6:

Control Perfectionism & CFS, and Find Your Inner Slob

Perfectionists are not obsessed with perfection. They are obsessed with imperfection. They look for imperfection all the time, and when it relates to them or their work, they will always find it.

You are probably wondering why I am putting Chronic Fatigue Syndrome (CFS) and perfectionism together. Well, let me tell you why. I have to admit that I know of no scientific evidence for there being a causal link, but it has been my experience over many years doing Radical Forgiveness workshops that at least 95% of those people who said they had experienced CFS were obsessive perfectionists. The connection has been increasingly difficult to ignore.

There are medical theories that suggest possible causes for CFS, but they seem tenuous at best or even spurious. People tend to bunch CFS in with a lot of other auto-immune related diseases. In the past some thought there might be a link between CFS and the Epstein Barr virus which is one of a variety of herpes viruses that is also responsible for inflicting mononucleosis or glandular fever on people, me included. I had a very bad case of it when I was about 6 or 7. It nearly killed me.

That said, I'll leave it to you to research the literature on the medical causes of CFS, if you feel so inclined, but I doubt you will find any reference to those who have it having an obsessive need to be a perfectionist. Nevertheless, based on my own observations, I maintain that the link is real. If there is someone out there who loves to do research and would care to do a proper statistical study to prove it one way or the other, I would love to hear from them.

But whether perfectionism is a cause of CFS or not doesn't really matter. What is important is that we offer a way for people to become free of the neurosis that is irrational perfectionism, since it is the cause of a great deal of stress and unhappiness. If by doing that we reduce the chances of a person developing CFS, so much the better.

I feel I should make a distinction here between a neurotic perfectionist and someone who sets incredibly high standards for themselves where it is important to have them. There is nothing wrong with the desire to do things really well and to the best of your ability. An artist-craftsman making some beautiful artifact, or a top tennis player might come to mind as being a perfectionist without being neurotic about it.

The neurosis only comes in when a person has to do absolutely everything perfectly, no matter what it is, even when it is not the least bit necessary. Perhaps their efforts are even counter-productive. They are devastated when the result is less than perfect, and they are never satisfied.

Some people are both. Steve Jobs demanded and got the very best from himself and those working for him because he had an extraordinary ability to create things that were as near perfect as it was possible to get at the time. He was obsessive about quality and had an incredible eye for aesthetic value in product design. His perfectionism took on a neurotic quality when it came to his own living environment.

He was so afraid of making a wrong decision when it came to furnishing his own house that he simply was unable to make choices. So he didn't. He lived in an extremely sparsely furnished and minimalist environment instead. He was unable to be satisfied with anything less than perfect and was unable to find it in any chair. That's crazy. But Jobs was special.

Actually, perfectionists are not obsessed with perfection – they are obsessed with *imperfection*. They look for imperfection all the time, and when it relates to them or their work, they will always find it. They are never happy with the result, nor with themselves. They always feel it could be better. Or that they could have been better. There's always more they could have done. It is never enough.

The core belief that sources the pain that every perfectionist feels is, "No matter how hard I try, I will never be enough." Not just that IT will never be enough, but they, as a person, will never be enough. Small wonder then that in the end, the body picks up on that and concludes, "Why bother? Why not just shut down and stop trying?" It wouldn't be surprising if chronic fatigue was a symptom of this core belief.

Could it be that their Higher Self is creating the condition of fatigue to teach the person that they have to heal that false core negative belief if they are to have a life? That's what I think.

Our body is always giving us messages but we seldom listen. We fail to realize that our bodies are connected to mind and spirit and that our physical body reflects in physical form the subconscious thoughts, beliefs and attitudes we have stored in our memories.

So where does that core negative belief come from and what can we do about it? Well, in almost every single case I find that the parents were responsible for inducing it in the child by never rewarding success and always demanding more. If the child got an A for a project at school, it should have been A+. If it was A+, "It better be an A+ next year as well then."

I read somewhere of a case where, after a young boy had won an important race at school, instead of celebrating it, his father could only say, "Yes, but you nearly lost, didn't you?"

Any child on the receiving end of such consistent wounding would eventually reach the conclusion that no matter how hard he or she tries, it will never be good enough for his parents. But children wounded in this way never seem to give up trying to win approval from their parents, no matter how old they get. I've had people in their 90's at my workshops still acting out that desire for their mother's or father's approval.

This is not to say that the parents were not loving and caring parents. In the main, I doubt they were intentionally trying to wound the child. They probably felt they were doing the right thing by 'encouraging' the child to do well and setting high standards for him or her to aspire to.

In societies like we have in America and to some extent England, where social mobility through hard work, education and the pursuit of excellence is seen as highly desirable, especially by a generation that had been denied it by virtue of their class, setting high level goals for children has always seemed to be of great importance. So, the kids have always been pushed to do better, be better and never be satisfied. Winning, too, has always been really important. Good enough has never been good enough.

But whether it was overt, misguided or totally unintended, this intense kind of mental and emotional conditioning is at the root of the neurosis we call perfectionism. The person is still trying to get their parents' approval. And it is painful in the extreme. The only way to medicate it is to go on and on trying to be perfect just to get approval from someone, even if it is not their parents. But that doesn't work either. They want it from their parents. No one else will do, and they will go on acting out that wound until the day they die unless they do something about it.

So, if this is you, what can you do about it? Well, the first thing is to realize that it is likely you will always be a perfectionist because that's who you are. If, in addition to having parents who were themselves perfectionists, which is invariably the case with people afflicted with the neurosis, you also happen to be born under the Sun sign Virgo, then you are even more likely to be an incurable perfectionist. If you are a triple Virgo, there's very little hope for you. I'm sorry.

I'm joking of course, but Virgos are naturally very detail-oriented and fussy people who always have to have everything nicely organized in its proper place, so it would definitely add to the obsession about being perfect if you are a Virgo.

But that aside, the beginning step is to love yourself being the perfectionist that you are. You simply have to accept yourself the way you are made. This is always the prerequisite for making any change in your life. If you make it wrong and try to change it from a place of judgment, you freeze the energy and nothing changes. What you resist, persists. As soon as you love something the way it is, you open up the energy for change to occur. It seems paradoxical, but that's how it works.

So do a Radical Self-Forgiveness/Self-Acceptance worksheet first. See if you can find peace in being the perfectionist that you are. You can at least begin to moderate your obsession, if not cure it altogether.

The next step is to use one of the Tipping Method tools to forgive your parents for making you into a perfectionist by withholding their love from you, never acknowledging your successes and for making you feel that no matter how hard you tried to please them, it would never be enough.

You could use a Radical Forgiveness worksheet, of course. But what happened to you as a child to make you a perfectionist may have been quite subtle. You may not have been aware of what was actually occurring. The pain of it was probably repressed anyway and largely forgotten. So it may be difficult for you to get in touch with the pain, the anger, the hurt and sadness just by doing a Radical Forgiveness worksheet. For these reasons, I think the Radical Forgiveness 3-Letter Process is a better option. It will take a bit more effort, but since perfectionism is so ingrained in you, I think it will be well worth it. The process is as follows.

Note: Even though I am explaining this process in the context of healing perfectionism, it can be used for any situation where you want to reach the stage of true forgiveness with someone. The letters are each written from a very different mind-set and exhibit a very different energy in each case, so I advise you to allow 24 hours to elapse between each one. **None of the three letters that you write in this process should ever be sent.**

LETTER #1

This letter is the easiest to write because, in essence, it is your victim story. In this case it will be about how your parents have ruined your life (always exaggerate in this letter) by making you into a perfectionist. They did it by withholding love from you, by always demanding more, never acknowledging you for what you did right, always raising the bar and never giving you the feeling that you were enough.

Let it all pour out in a torrent of accusatory and even vengeful language. Don't censor it in any way. Just let it rip, and let them know just how much they have damaged you and hurt you, etc. You make no excuses for them and show no mercy whatsoever. All you know is that you are the victim in this situation. Vent all your anger and rage in this letter. Hold nothing back. You can threaten vengeance of the vilest kind if it makes you feel good. Keep writing until you have nothing left to say. Get everything out. It might take many pages.

The process of writing this letter often causes people to shed a lot of tears – tears of rage, sadness, resentment and hurt. Let them flow if this happens for you. Have a box of tissues beside you. If you are angry, scream into a pillow or do some physical activity to help you feel your anger. *But, remember, under no circumstances are you to mail this letter!*

LETTER #2

This is a much more difficult letter to write and requires you to be in a more reflective frame of mind, which is best done the next day after you have cooled down somewhat and slept on it. It allows a dream cycle to occur between each letter so each one can be processed by the subconscious mind. That said, don't go more than two days between writing the first and second letters.

Whereas the first letter expresses the raw victim story, this second one is where you reduce the amount of energy invested in the story by coming to the realization that while your *pain* is in what actually happened, the *suffering* (in this case perfectionism) was in how you might have expanded the story by making a lot of erroneous interpretations about what your parents were communicating to you.

This letter, therefore, should help you sort out what is or was true versus what you imagined was true. In that sense, this part of this letter might become something of a dialogue with yourself about what happened as if you were musing about the whole thing, trying to make some sense of it, stripping out and noting down everything you made up about the story that was just not true.

The second part of Letter #2 is going to resemble what we would normally expect to be the sentiment expressed with the best of traditional forgiveness. Because you don't let the person off the hook, it is still firmly based in victim consciousness. However, it does ask you to be more conciliatory, understanding and empathetic, and to cut the person some slack. It also asks that you put yourself in their shoes and imagine whether you might have done the same had you been in a similar circumstance or frame of mind.

You might need to take into account their upbringing and life experiences. For example, your parents may have come from a very impoverished background and fought hard to provide you with the opportunity to have a better life than they did. This may have made them more extreme in their expectations of you. The task in this letter, then, is to do your best to bring humility, tolerance, understanding and compassion to the situation – even if at this time you are not actually feeling it.

LETTER #3
While the first two letters will be expressions of your authentic thoughts and feelings, this third letter will not be. It will be a 'fake-it-till-you-make-it,' attempt at a reframe. You have to write it as if you believe it totally, with as much fervor and skill as you used for the previous two letters. With this one, you will feel as if you are a fraud. It doesn't matter; your body will get it.

In this letter, you attempt to describe a new interpretation of the situation based on the principles of Radical Forgiveness. In other words, you write that you now realize the person was, at the soul level, acting out of love by doing what he/she did because it was what you (your soul) wanted to experience. You had, in fact, recruited him/her to do it, not TO you, but FOR you.

It is even likely that you and the other person had agreed up front, prior to incarnation, that he/she would provide this experience for you — a soul contract in other words. All you are now able to feel towards this person is gratitude.

Follow this up by listening to *The Wake for the Inner Child Meditation.* In this meditation you allow the wounded inner child to give up its need for his/her parents' approval and to die peacefully at last. Listening to this meditation will help you to mentally and emotionally resolve to give up your need for your parent's approval. You are never going to get it in the way you wanted it as a child, even if they are still alive and are proud of you now. It's not the same, and it doesn't heal that childhood wound. But having done the Radical Forgiveness work and seen the perfection in the situation, you can now, as an adult, stop needing what they can never give you. It's your need for it that caused the pain. You no longer need it, because you can now give that approval to yourself.

The last step is to make a determination never to do to your own children (if you have any, or plan to have them) what your parents did to you. Love and accept them for who they are. Encourage them of course, but don't push too hard, and give them praise when they do well.

Finally, you have to practice being a non-perfectionist. As I pointed out earlier, perfectionism is almost incurable, but you can get to the point where you are not obsessive about it. You can perhaps actually find satisfaction in being more relaxed and less self-critical about what you do and how you feel about yourself.

I always recommend putting aside some hours or even a day a week where you intentionally allow yourself to be a lot less than perfect. Not quite a slob, but going in that direction. Let your 'inner slob" come out for a bit.

For example, try not washing the dishes right away. If you never leave the house without make-up, go out without it. Don't check your e-mails for half a day at least. Switch off your cell phone. Don't return texts or phone calls. Don't make the bed. But do it all consciously and with full awareness of how it feels. It will create anxiety at first, but push through it.

Something else you might try is to get some paints like the ones kids use at school and do some paintings freestyle. Try finger painting even. If you have kids, do it with them. Refuse to be limited by having to stay within lines or do things 'properly.' Be sure to put your paintings up where you can see them and leave them there for all to see for at least two days. They do not need to look good, pretty or like any work of art at all. Just free expression.

Finally, follow up periodically with the 13 Steps to Radical Self-Forgiveness and the 13 Steps to Self-Acceptance.

RESOURCES FOR THIS APPLICATION: (Details in the Resources Section at the back of this book and at www.radicalforgiveness.com.)

Book: *Radical Forgiveness*

Worksheets:
Radical Forgiveness Worksheet
Radical Self-Forgiveness/Acceptance Worksheet

Audios:
A Wake for the Inner Child Meditation
13 Steps to Self Forgiveness
13 Steps to Radical Forgiveness
Radical Self Forgiveness Practices (CD)

Videos:
Radical Self-Forgiveness and Self-Acceptance

Application #7:

Overcome Your Addiction with RF as the Next Step

*Radical Forgiveness is the vital next Step.
It transforms the process from being
shame-based to Love-based.*

L et me say right away that I think the 12-Step Recovery
approach to dealing with addictions is the best overall
approach we have at this time, and I am sure it was
divinely inspired. I think the proof of that lies in the fact that
it has been going all these years without having any power
structure, no leader, no management system and no money
being made from it. The sponsorship system is the best and
most generous example of compassion in action I've seen.

That said, I do think there is a need for a further Step,
which would, of course, be Radical Forgiveness. I don't
think it would necessarily come at the end, but it needs to
go in somewhere in order to free people from the victim
consciousness that seems to me inherent in all 12-step
programs. Radical Forgiveness would turn the process from
being essentially shame-based to Love-based.

It would probably be best used with or before Step 4, which
is where most people get stuck and few get beyond. This is
where they are asked to take a moral inventory of all their
defects. Most addicts have been deeply shamed at some point
in their lives and have survived by using alcohol, drugs, sex,
food, gambling and other ways to numb that pain. It is asking

a great deal of them to bring all that deeply repressed shame to the surface without a great deal of support and some powerful tools. For most it is just too painful. So they stop there and just become addicted to meetings instead. Very few people get to complete all 12 steps.

Even those very experienced with 12-step programs, with many years of sobriety under their belts, can get stuck in victim consciousness without being aware of it. I have told this story before elsewhere, but it is worth telling here because it illustrates this point really well.

Mike (not his real name) was telling a friend of mine over dinner that he was spending most of his time these days sponsoring people in the AA program. He had made it a very big part of his life. He shared that he had been able to let go of his addiction 14 years before after realizing he had been sexually abused as a baby by his mother, and was using alcohol to medicate the pain. Once he became acquainted with the pain, he had been able to stop drinking. He then made this statement: "But you know, I will never be free of my addiction until I know why she did it." To which I responded, "Then you are screwed, aren't you?"

He was very shocked and demanded to know why I said that. I replied, "You are making your healing contingent upon getting an answer to an unanswerable question. She didn't know why she did it any more than you know. No one knows why. And in any case, 'why' is a victim's question. That's why you are screwed. You are still giving your power away to your mother and you are still afraid of your pain."

"So what do you suggest?" he said sarcastically. "Hang out in a different question," I replied. "Such as, 'I wonder what the gift might have been in having had my mother do that to me?' It's an equally unanswerable question but a much better question to hang out in than the other one. This one will free you from your addiction, whereas the other disempowers you and keeps you tied to your addiction."

He didn't like it, but the next day I got a phone call from him. "I have been up all night thinking about what you said, and I get it. You have saved my life. Thank you."

So the way out of an addiction is to first find out what pain is being medicated by the substance or experience of choice, and then to use the tools of Radical Forgiveness to release the pain. It really is that simple.

The Amends
I imagine that Radical Forgiveness would also be of great assistance to those who get to Step 9, which asks them to make amends to people they have harmed. Doing some Radical Self-Forgiveness and Self-Acceptance beforehand would give it greater meaning and more authenticity. That's because they would be doing it, not out of a sense of obligation, but with a different consciousness – more from their heart, with a great deal of love and gratitude for the person they are apologizing to. It would make the difference between making a Radical Apology instead of an ordinary Apology. Let me explain.

The Ordinary Apology: This recognizes that someone was hurt, disadvantaged or in some other way damaged because of something we intentionally did – and that

87

what we did was wrong. It is a direct communication to the aggrieved party that we are in sorrow, guilt and regret that the event occurred, and we wish the party to know this. It may also be an appeal for forgiveness. However, because there is no recognition of any underlying spiritual purpose in what took place, victim consciousness is fully maintained. This kind of apology is not compatible with Radical Forgiveness and is relatively shallow.

The Radical Apology: This recognizes that, in human terms, someone got hurt. It is something about which we feel true sorrow and perhaps even 'appropriate' guilt. We also accept full responsibility for what happened in human and worldly terms and are willing to be accountable for what we have done. At the same time, however, we are open to the possibility that some higher purpose was being served, and it had to happen that way for whatever reason. We are, in effect, seeing the situation from the perspective of both the World of Spirit and the World of Humanity at the same time. This has the effect of raising our own vibration while releasing the low vibration energy tied up in the situation itself. This enables healing to occur for all concerned, as well as a general raising of consciousness, ensuring that in the future there will be less need for such hurtful things to occur.

However, since it is still difficult for us – as the perpetrator – to really 'know' that there was a perfection in the situation, it seems that a genuine expression of compassion and sorrow (rather than regret), might help us both, as this might be even more difficult for the victim. The sorrow is not so much because it happened, but that the person (a human being) was hurt or damaged. If nothing else, it opens the energy up for Radical Forgiveness to enter into play — especially for the victim. Therefore a Radical Apology is a BRIDGE to Radical Forgiveness and Reconciliation. It is also a preliminary step in the direction of clearing one's shadow, which is really what Step Four is all about and why most people find it so frightening.

The big difference with Radical Forgiveness is that the person to whom you are expressing your amends *would not need to know* that you are holding what happened any differently from the normal perception of what happened – YOU WOULD NOT TELL THEM. But it will make a difference to your energy, and he or she is likely to feel it subconsciously. It is also likely to make a difference on whether or not the amends is accepted.

I am actually quite skeptical about the advisability of making 'regular apology' amends at all for long-ago hurts, and the bigger the harm done, the more skeptical I am. In many cases, 'amends' are done in such a way that the person feels they are being manipulated and dumped on. The person doing the amends step may feel better for having unloaded their guilt, but the victim feels a lot worse for having been reminded of the pain they endured at the time and may have put to bed a long time ago. The victim may feel the perpetrator is victimizing them all over again by making them feel guilty if they are not ready to forgive.

For that reason, I believe people should think long and hard before they do the amends process with the person they hurt. If there is any doubt at all as to how it might land for the receiving person, they should find an alternative. Doing it with a surrogate may be one alternative.

If one does the Radical Self-Forgiveness process on oneself first, and then, in solitude, goes into the heart and asks in a genuinely prayerful manner for forgiveness from the other person and from oneself, that is much more effective than doing the amends as "a process." It leaves the other person out of it completely, has no potential to re-injure the victim, and will have a much more profound effect for both of you. Moreover, it can be done many times over as a meditation until such time as it feels complete.

What I have seen, ironically, is that the person to whom the amends would otherwise have been directed will feel the shift in energy. Often the person offers their forgiveness quite spontaneously and without prompting. It is quite amazing how this happens, and is far more healing for the victim (and for you) if they come to a place of forgiveness on their own.

If you are in a 12 Step Recovery program I suggest you familiarize yourself with the process of Radical Forgiveness and Radical Self-Forgiveness. Discuss it with your sponsor so he or she knows what you are doing and is in alignment with it.

My wish for you is that, through Radical Forgiveness, you will not only be free of the pain underlying the need for the addictive behavior, but free of the addiction itself. If you then choose to sponsor people, I would hope you would introduce them to Radical Forgiveness so they, too, have the next step.

RESOURCES FOR THIS APPLICATION:
(Details in the Resources Section at the back of this book and at www.radicalforgiveness.com.)

Book: *Radical Forgiveness*

Worksheet: Radical Self-Forgiveness/Self-Acceptance

Application #8:

Release That Trauma and Let's Get On With Life

It saddens me that so many people remain burdened by a trauma all their lives, even after awakening, just because they have not had the chance to see it from the Radical Forgiveness perspective.

The high rate of suicide among soldiers returning from the wars in Iraq and Afghanistan is an indication of how overwhelming trauma can be. Who wouldn't be traumatized, being shot at all the time and threatened by bombs and roadside IEDs that might take off your legs and arms? These psychological wounds can be just as bad as artillery fire. The unrelenting emotional pain and the feeling of helplessness that goes along with it, even after coming home, are so great that death must have seemed to be the only way out for those soldiers.

This is all the more tragic if you consider the fact that it is highly likely that, once they get to the other side, they'll find they have taken their pain with them and nothing has changed. (See Application #21.) But no one tells them that. Doing Radical Forgiveness to release the pain while still here on this side is a much better option. I just wish it could be made more available to the veterans of these terrible wars who are hurting so badly. Maybe it will soon.

Of course, there are many ways, other than war, in which we can become traumatized, especially when we are children.

Trauma is caused by events that destroy our sense of security, and/or our trust in everyone around us and even threaten our lives. The more fear involved, the more intense the trauma is likely to be. It can be caused by a one-time event like a car crash, a natural disaster or a violent attack. Sexual abuse is almost always traumatic. Trauma can also come from being in an ongoing, highly stressful situation, such as living with an abusive dysfunctional family, living in a crime-ridden area or fighting a cancer diagnosis. The sudden death of a loved one can be very traumatic, too, which is why we have created an online program designed to reduce the suffering that people otherwise have to endure.

We all have natural defense mechanisms that help us cope with the shock and the fear experienced in traumatic situations. Denial is one example. Going out of body or dissociating is another. Suppression of the emotional pain or 'numbing out' with addiction works well temporarily too. Some people come out of it after using these mechanisms for a while. Others don't. They become depressed and exhibit mental and behavioral problems. This then becomes identified as post-traumatic stress syndrome.

Repression is another defense mechanism. This is used when the trauma is more severe; the mind just cannot handle it, so it just blocks it out. The pain and the memory buried deep in the unconscious mind is totally out of conscious awareness. The danger with this one is that it can become all but permanent. It still has energy attached to it as well, though, so if something a bit like the original event unexpectedly triggers it, the person is likely to become re-traumatized, often with devastating results.

We know from what we have discussed already that such traumas could possibly have been what the soul created for its learning. In that sense, there was a spiritual purpose to it. However, since our conversation here is about how life should be lived after the Awakening, we are focusing on the role of Radical Forgiveness Therapy to help people heal the trauma, not leverage it. Our Higher Self took care of that part some time ago.

That phase being over, it now becomes necessary to use Radical Forgiveness Therapy to help you wean yourself off those defense mechanisms. These would have been helpful to you in the beginning, but may have become debilitating and semi-permanent ways of being. Of course, if you have been severely traumatized and have not yet come out of it you should seek qualified professional help. However, let me explain why I think Radical Forgiveness Therapy should be at least part of your protocol. If your trauma was or is less severe and you are functional, it might well be sufficient. Let me explain why.

The first step in any process of dealing with a trauma is to find a way to talk about what happened. It is the same with Radical Forgiveness. But with traditional therapy, being able to talk about it may take a long time and might need a lot of patience on the part of the therapist. In this situation, you would need to feel very safe and emotionally supported. You would need to feel totally understood and validated. Certainly not judged. You would need to feel the person listening has empathy with your story and is not trying to fix you.

95

The more you talk, the more the tension is released from your mind and body. Being encouraged to focus on body sensations as you talk gets you more in touch with the memories and feelings you experienced at the time, as well as those you experience as you relate your story. (Feeling the feelings is the second step in the Radical Forgiveness process.)

Cognitive therapy often ignores the fact that the energy induced by the trauma gets trapped in the body. When I was practicing hypnotherapy, I had occasion to work with someone who was involved in a very serious car crash. After he had related as much of the story he could remember, which was actually very little, I put him into a hypnotic trance and had him draw on body memory by going very slowly and deliberately through the movements that his body made at the moment of impact. I also asked him to describe what was going on in his body as he was going through the motions.

This had the effect of releasing the energy from all parts of his body that had been injured. It had held both the physical and emotional memory of the entire event. Not only did the memory of what happened come back, so he could talk about it with clarity, his body straightened and the pain he had come in with began to abate. This technique is called Somatic Healing. As the name implies, it employs the body's ability to heal itself.

Another technique that was developed by Francine Shapiro in 1989 to treat PTSD/PTSS was the technique known as Eye Movement Desensitization and Reprocessing (EMDR). This involved the therapist asking the person to look at and follow his moving finger so that the veteran's eyes were continually going back and forth from side to side while conversing. This, too, seemed to have the effect of releasing energy. While the reason for its effectiveness is still not completely understood, it works. Its efficacy is related to connecting and stimulating the two halves of the brain. The right hemisphere has no facility for language but is good at seeing patterns and thinking holistically, while the left hemisphere has language and is more linear, rational and analytical. So the lateral movements of the eyes link the two halves and enable the person to speak about the event from a right brain perspective with language generated from the left.

Virtual Reality technology is also being used with great success to desensitize the trauma by having the person wear the headgear and to re-experience all the sights, sounds and smells associated with the trauma.

One of the effects of having some of the defense mechanisms made permanent is that the person numbs out. They can't feel their feelings. It's not that the feelings are not there. The person is simply unable to access them. Again, doing something physical helps them discharge pent-up "fight-or-flight" energy – something explosive and fast moving like beating some cushions with a tennis racquet. (It makes such a good noise!) Again the body takes over. The mind gets out of the way and the resistance to feeling the feelings dissolves. The anger erupts. The person collapses in tears, shakes violently for a few minutes and then goes quiet. Then come the feelings beneath the anger – sadness, grief, hurt and very often, survivor's remorse. "Why was I spared when my mates were killed? It should have been me."

97

Beating the cushion is a technique I use all the time in Radical Forgiveness Therapy. You have to get in touch with the raw emotion behind what happened.

As I have said previously, you cannot heal what you don't feel. That's especially true when there is real trauma involved. But I never recommend that someone do it on their own without having support from someone who can hold the space for them to go through their anger and the whole process without needing to intervene or being fazed by the process. It is not always pretty and can be upsetting to someone who is not used to it.

As you know, the 3rd stage in the Radical Forgiveness Process is collapsing the story. This is where the purpose would be to take some of the heat out of the trauma by trying to rationalize it, understand why it happened, how they might have contributed to the situation (while avoiding inappropriate guilt), what factors might have made it inevitable, and so on. If there were others involved who might have caused the trauma, it can help to see it from their point of view and try to understand how events might have led them to make that mistake or take that action.

This is cognitive therapy pure and simple, and for most people who have been traumatized, this is the end of the road. There's nowhere else to go. It works well enough for many even though it takes a great deal of time and money and in my view probably leaves a lot undone.

Taking it to the next level, to that of Radical Forgiveness, the person is introduced to the idea that what happened was supposed to happen that way and that, far from being a tragedy, it was what their Higher Self had set up for them to experience. That's when the healing process really takes off and goes into overdrive.

However, the timing has to be right. The Radical Forgiveness reframe has to be introduced carefully and with due respect for the person's existing consciousness at the time. If it is proposed too early, the person can be re-traumatized. The idea that they created it and that, from a spiritual perspective, it was entirely perfect might be just too radical.

My approach, when I have done all the emotional work and have completed the cognitive analysis and feel the person is ready, goes something like this: "Would you possibly be open to seeing this situation from a different perspective?" If I sense curiosity coming back from them, I then launch into it, step by step, looking to see how it might be landing for them.

I never ask them to believe it. In fact, I usually say, "I don't believe it myself, but something happens if we just become willing to believe it. So, for a moment let's just suppose..." And I go from there. They nearly always buy it. Tentatively at first, of course, but gradually they find a sense of rightness about it. It resonates. They notice that they feel different inside. A weight has lifted from them. They become alive again.

My main experience over the years has been with people traumatized through sexual abuse and other relationship-based traumas, as well as those having lost someone in tragic circumstances. But no matter whether a person has been traumatized by a car accident, a severe injury, or a breakup of a relationship so difficult they can't move on... when people in any way feel they are unable to have a normal life because of what happened to them, I am totally convinced that Radical Forgiveness Therapy is at least part of the answer.

It saddens me that so many people remain burdened by a trauma all their lives, even after awakening, just because they haven't been given the chance to see it from the Radical Forgiveness perspective. I hope this will change when we all start to wake up to this truth.

If you are caring for someone who has been traumatized and is suffering from Post-Traumatic Stress Syndrome, you will need a lot of patience and understanding if your relationship is to survive. Resist the urge to put pressure on them to talk. Just be there for them as best you can.

However, if you do want to take it to the next level, my advice is if you don't already have the book *Radical Forgiveness,* get yourself a copy. Read it thoroughly, and if it resonates with you and you think it might help the person who is traumatized, casually leave the book around where it might be seen but not too obviously 'planted.'

Say nothing about it. As time goes on he/she may pick it up and start reading it. Don't mention it unless he/she does. It may be a long while before this happens, so be patient. The person's Higher Self will know when the time has arrived for him or her to pick it up.

Until then, you have to just wait. Spirit will handle the details when the time is right, so surrender is the name of the game for you. In the meantime, you can use the tools yourself in order to stay centered.

If he or she goes for it, I would suggest a Miracles Workshop or a few private sessions with a Radical Forgiveness Therapy Practitioner as the best options. Just doing a worksheet is probably not going to be enough.

RESOURCES FOR THIS APPLICATION: (Details in the Resources Section at the back of this book and at www.radicalforgiveness.com.)

Book: *Radical Forgiveness*
Workshop: *"Miracles" Workshop*
Radical Forgiveness Therapy

Application #9:

Manage Anger and Other Juicy Emotions

Anger is a secondary emotion and as such is usually sitting on top of another emotion like hurt, sadness, jealousy, fear, resentment, disappointment, etc. Anger is used as a way to cover up the real pain and protect the heart.

Anger scares people. Men especially are frightened of it because they fear they might lose control and hurt someone if they allow themselves to really feel it. Knowing how to control one's anger without denying it or suppressing it is, therefore, of paramount importance. Radical Forgiveness can help. Let me explain how.

The best working definition of an emotion is a thought attached to a feeling. Which comes first depends on the type of stimulus, but my guess is that in most cases it is the thought that causes the chemical reactions in the body that we register as the feeling.

Yes, I do concede there are times when we get a feeling in the body and then make some attempt to attach meaning to it, but I believe this is the body acting as an intuitive messaging system. When we get the message and convert it to a thought, this might then trigger an emotion.

Anyway, for the sake of simplicity, let's assume it happens as follows. First comes perception. We then mentally process

103

what we perceive and develop a thought based not just on what is there, but also on what we already know, what we believe, what our previous experience has been, what our attitudes and prejudices are and so on. Then comes the feeling and then, if required, action. And it all happens in a flash.

The emotion is the result of cause and effect. The thoughts are the cause and the feelings are the effect. The feelings themselves happen automatically and are beyond our control. What we do have dominion over, however, since they are the cause, are our thoughts.

This means the key to managing our emotions is to consciously monitor what passes through our mind. Then, be open to thinking in ways that will reduce the likelihood of these emotions causing a violent or extreme emotional response like rage, terror or shame.

The most obvious cause of strong feelings bringing out our worst emotional response is the belief system we have come to know as victim consciousness. If we believe we are always the victim in every situation, and other people are responsible for our discomfort in every unpleasant situation that occurs, then anger will almost always be our default response. We will feel justified in feeling this way and very self-righteous.

If, on the other hand, we are grounded in the Radical Forgiveness philosophy that says we are always accountable for what happens in our lives, and that, in spite of how things appear, nothing wrong or right is happening, then our emotional response will, given a little cooling down time perhaps, be very different.

Now, this is not to say that we, as ordinary human beings, will not have the kind of response that most people have when 'shit happens,' but as we process the event in our minds, the Radical Forgiveness idea will come to be part of the mix and will begin to modify our response. At that point 'shift happens.' Transformation occurs.

But between the 'shit happens' and the 'shift happens,' when we are still feeling like victims, and have yet to cool down, we may have to manage the anger that arises in the moment. You do this in four stages.

Stage 1: Recognize the Feeling. Acknowledge to yourself that you are angry. Bear in mind that anger is a secondary emotion and is usually sitting on top of another emotion, such as hurt, sadness, jealousy, fear, resentment, disappointment, etc. Anger is used as a way to cover up the real pain and protect the heart. So, if you are aware, you might be able to identify the emotion under the anger. If not, that's OK. Just feel what you can feel.

Stage 2: Accept the feeling. Be OK with the feeling and love yourself for having it. You are a human being and it is natural that you feel anger in this moment. Do not judge it. Remember, there is no such thing as a negative emotion. It only becomes negative when you deny, suppress or repress it. Emotions give you feedback about whether you are lowering or raising your vibration, so they all serve a good purpose. They cover a wide range from utter despair to perfect bliss, and we are all given the capacity to feel them all. Who are we to say that any one of them is bad?

Stage 3: Delay the Expression of the Feeling. This may not be necessary. If it is OK to express it in the moment, go ahead and do so. If, on the other hand, it would not be appropriate, delay the expression of it until it is safe to let it go.

Stage 4: Express How You Feel. Find a safe way to get the feelings out of your body by doing something physical, like speaking it out, crying, shouting, beating cushions, chopping wood or any kind of activity. It helps if you have someone with you to be a witness.

If Stage 3 is not necessary, the whole process might only take a few minutes. Should it be necessary, it could take a while. But please do not use this as an excuse to avoid expressing it. That would be denial of it, and that's what makes it toxic.

Now, to get back to 'shift happens.' The secret to making that transition happen is, once again, the Emerge-n-See 4-Step process. As you know, this is to be used right at the moment something upsetting happens or, in this case, immediately after having completed at least Stages One and Two of the above anger management process, or after Stage Four if the third one was not necessary.

Let me remind you once again of the four statements. Even if you have already committed them to memory, it helps to write them out on a business card you keep in your wallet or purse.

1. Look What I've Created
2. I Notice My Judgments and Feelings But Love Myself Anyway
3. I Am Willing to See the Perfection in the Situation
4. I Choose Peace

In Step One, you are taking responsibility for co-creating the situation. In Step Two, you are acknowledging that you are a human being with feelings and the need to judge the situation. Step Three is the actual Radical Forgiveness step in which you are expressing your willingness to see the perfection, while in Step Four you make a choice to change your feeling tone from anger to peace. Keep repeating these four steps in your head until the peace becomes real. At that point the shift will have occurred and your anger will have been transformed. In all likelihood the situation itself will have resolved itself too.

RESOURCES FOR THIS APPLICATION:
(Details in the Resources Section at the back of this book and at www.radicalforgiveness.com.)

Worksheet: *Radical Forgiveness*
Audio: Radical Forgiveness Meditations

---

25 Practical Uses for Radical Forgiveness:
Solving the Problems and Challenges
of Everyday Life in a New Way

PART TWO

An Application for Dispute Resolution

10. Resolve Disputes, Win Law Suits and Ace Court Cases

Application #10:

Resolve Disputes, Win Lawsuits and Ace Court Cases

When they enter the courtroom or engage in settlement negotiations around a table, I want them to be in a state of high vibration emanating the energy of Love and totally surrendered to the outcome. After that, it's up to Spirit.

Disputes with neighbors, authorities and others who disrupt our peace and bring varying degrees of stress into our lives can be very challenging. Our usual way of dealing with such problems is to go on the defensive and perhaps even mount some sort of counter-attack. Worst case scenario, we may get drawn into a lawsuit and have to endure subsequent court proceedings.

Of course, you may have very little choice but to engage in the fight and do all you can to defend yourself against whoever is trying to impose their will on you. I can tell you from experience that if you do what you have to do with the right energy, generated easily through Radical Forgiveness, the outcome will be very different.

You might even cause the dispute to collapse entirely and become resolved to everyone's satisfaction. Even if that doesn't happen, you can come out of the experience with a lot more peace of mind than if you had not applied Radical Forgiveness to the situation.

111

Recently my daughter Lorraine experienced being bullied at work. She is a very experienced and highly qualified nurse, but at work she was being constantly harassed and bullied by a supervisor who had recently been assigned to her section. It was very upsetting to Lorraine, and it was making her feel bad and very unhappy. She made a formal complaint against the supervisor, but at the preliminary hearing she became quite emotional and upset, and she was seriously considering quitting her position.

I suggested she take the Radical Forgiveness approach to the situation. After discussing it, she did several worksheets on the supervisor. When she went to the next hearing, her union representative said he couldn't believe how composed and strong she was compared to the previous time. She seemed a wholly different person. She did not say anything derogatory about the supervisor, just reported the facts. The Board was very sympathetic to her case and everything went well.

The wheels of justice turn slowly in such organizations as the National Health Service, but in time the bullying stopped. Sometime later, Lorraine was offered a new and better job in a different hospital. It suited her needs exactly because it offered her flexibility with hours. She is in training to be certified as a Reflexologist and a Radical Living Coach and needed total flexibility in how many hours she would work at the hospital so she can build her practice. It was all perfect. But without the Radical Forgiveness process, she would probably still be doing full time at the other hospital, and in all likelihood, still fighting against her supervisor.

112

Radical Forgiveness works at many different levels and employs a variety of energies. We use our intellect to create a meaningful context for what is happening or has happened. That's mental energy. Secondly, we use our emotional energy to feel into the situation and bring feelings into play as part of the experience. Thirdly, we use spiritual energy to bring Love to the situation. All three energies are brought forth by doing the worksheets.

Seen in this light, then, it becomes clear that Radical Forgiveness is essentially an energy experience. That's why it works virtually instantaneously and irrespective of distance.

We know that human beings are connected energetically. When one person shifts their energy, it has an effect on those to whom we are most strongly connected at the time. Obviously, the strongest energetic connections tend to be between family members, friends and lovers. Identical twins are so connected at the energetic level, they exhibit seemingly magical synchronicity of mind and emotion, whether or not they are in physical proximity.

But circumstances can draw people together into a similar network of connectivity as well. Rupert Sheldrake, the English biologist, has coined the term morphogenetic fields to describe the existence of energy fields that are self-organizing and self-regulating systems that sustain patterns of vibratory or rhythmic activity. Elements are attracted to each other by morphic resonance to create fields which are constantly changing and evolving. When one element in the field changes, this affects the whole field and it responds by changing too.

The concept is applicable at all levels, from quantum phenomena to social group behavior. For example, such fields are created when people with some common interest or shared group experience become strongly connected, such as with a club, a sports team, or a business. Through morphic resonance, each individual becomes affected by the energy of the others in the group.

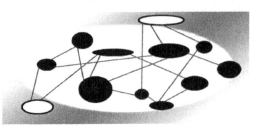

Fig. 7: *Morphogenetic fields*

These morphic fields link individual members through extrasensory and energetic resonance (consciousness), a process that is independent of time and space. This is why, when someone forgives using Radical Forgiveness, the effect is felt immediately by the person being forgiven no matter how far away they are, or how long ago the event took place.

But we need to understand that the effects can be positive or negative depending on your energy, your interest and your influence within the field. If there are one or two people within the field emanating negative energy, such as hatred, vengefulness, spite, etc., this will have a big effect on the overall energy field and it will affect the outcome accordingly.

As I describe in my book, *Radical Forgiveness*, I was once asked to address the National Society of Mediators at their annual conference. I was only to have about 45 minutes and they were to be eating lunch while listening to me! I went early to listen in on their discussions in order to get a feel for their way of thinking. I determined that, in terms of background, about 50% of the attendees were lawyers and 50% were counselors, and that their commitment to mediation left them fairly open-minded and flexible in their approaches to problem solving.

For the first twenty minutes or so, I did my best to explain the concepts and assumptions underlying Radical Forgiveness. Then I drew the following diagram (next page) to represent the energetic relationship between them and their clients.

I then put it to them that their perception of the situation they were mediating was likely to be that what was happening to Clients A and B was unfortunate at best and a tragedy at worst. I also said that the people most closely connected to them (family, children, business partners, etc.) would also be the victims if the decision went against either A or B.

I also described their role as mediator, as trying to make the best of a bad situation and resolve it in a way that would be the least damaging to both parties and their dependents. But there would likely to be one of the parties who felt they had lost and would still feel embittered.

115

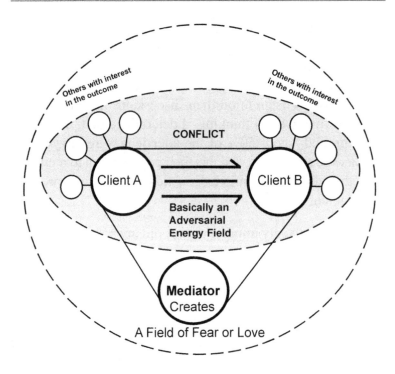

Fig. 8: *The Mediation Field*

They agreed that this was a fair characterization of their task and that the energy field around the situation for the clients was one of overt hostility and mistrust between the parties. Had it been otherwise, they wouldn't have needed them to mediate.

Then I factored their own energy into the situation. They saw that their energy field would normally contain thoughts and feelings related to the perception that this was a "bad" situation. I also suggested that, even though they were trying to mediate and help both clients, their perception of the situation as "bad" fed into the clients' energy field and reinforced their victim consciousness.

"What if," I asked then, "instead of seeing this situation as tragic and undesirable, you became willing to entertain the idea that this was a Divine plan unfolding exactly as it needed to unfold, and that each of the parties, including the ones on the periphery, were actually getting exactly what they subconsciously wanted at the soul level – and that this was true no matter how this situation worked out?

"Do you think that would make a difference? Your energy field, instead of being filled with fear-based thoughts and emotions, would be filled with love. Do you think that would have an effect on how the situation would finally be resolved?"

Surprisingly, they understood. Even the lawyers got it! There was broad acceptance of the idea that how they held the situation in their own minds was a powerful factor in determining how the situation came out. It was not that anything would be done differently or overtly changed. It would just be that by holding the idea that everything was perfect, the energy would be allowed to move, without as much resistance, in whatever direction it needed to move.

117

That is what transforming energy through Radical Forgiveness means. But it takes the use of all three forms of energy to make it happen. Mental energy to bring conscious awareness to the situation and a sharp mind in the use of language and persuasion. Emotional energy that when projected out to everyone makes people feel acknowledged, understood and empathized with, even while you may have to be tough in your negotiations. Then spiritual energy unites everyone at the heart level as you project Love into the situation. Love is the strongest of all energies and will overcome any amount of negative energy that is present in the field. Love transforms.

That said, there is a caveat to all this. It will not work if, in your heart of hearts, you know that your case is not just, and you are simply using Radical Forgiveness to abrogate responsibility, deny criminality or avoid accountability. You will be so out of integrity that your spirit will not allow you to project Love into the situation. You will simply project fear. Your only remedy in that case is to do the Radical Self-Forgiveness process on yourself, and then come to the situation with due humility and acceptance. Only then will you be able to have a positive effect on the situation from a vibratory standpoint.

From a practical point of view then, assuming you have just cause to feel victimized by the dispute situation, here's what you need to do. First identify all the players who seem to be ranged against you. If it is a neighbor, for example, it might only be one person, a couple or a family group. As soon as you become aware of the issue brewing, do a Radical Forgiveness worksheet immediately on each of the players, even while you try to resolve the situation with them at the human level.

Do your best to hold the Love vibration and not get drawn into the opposite vibration. Own your own feelings, and resist the desire to lay blame. Hopefully, this will dissolve the dispute before the energies become fixed and positions become hardened. If not, just keep holding onto the idea that there is perfection in there somewhere. You co-created the situation with this person for a reason, therefore a healing opportunity is contained in there somewhere.

Keep doing the four steps in your mind. Let me remind you again what they are:

1. Look What I Created!

2. I Notice My Feelings and My Judgments but Love Myself Anyway.

3. I Am Willing to See the Perfection in the Situation.

4. I Choose Peace.

If your dispute is with an authority like the police, the government, debt collection agency, a hospital, or any kind of organization, you may have to do the worksheets on the 'faceless' organization itself if there is no one person to focus on and everything is done by e-mail or letters. It is better if you can find an individual who represents that organization, but if not, do your best to personalize it in some way, so that when you do the Radical Forgiveness Worksheets you have some kind of identity to work with in your own mind and on whom to do your best to project Love. It's not easy to project love onto a faceless organization, but Radical Forgiveness is

119

a 'fake-it-till-you-make-it' proposition anyway, so do it the best you can. It still works.

I went through a bankruptcy myself once, and by using this process, formed a good working relationship with the person from the debt collection agency who at first was calling me almost every day. After a while, they backed off and gave me the space I needed to resolve my financial situation. Going through that experience taught me a lot about the power of love to transform any situation. I did worksheets on the bankruptcy attorneys and the partner I was in business with who turned out to be a criminal, plus a lot of self-forgiveness worksheets on myself for creating that situation. It all worked out.

If you ever have to come to court to defend yourself, it might be easier in one sense to energetically affect what happens. That's because most, if not all, the players are present in the courtroom.

On the other hand, it is pretty easy to become so overwhelmed and fearful in that situation that you are unable to keep your vibration high.

Nevertheless, even if this happens, you will have done a lot of worksheets prior to the hearing, so that energy will be in the courtroom anyway. But if you are able to stay in a state of peace, perhaps even grace, and focus on just feeling love in your heart for every person in the room, Spirit will take care of the rest for you. That's because the worksheet is a form of secular prayer and represents a request for help from the spiritual realm.

I'm not saying, of course, that you will always get the result you want, because from a spiritual standpoint it might not be in your soul's interest. Your Higher Self may have different ideas about what is best for you. So, be ready to surrender to whatever happens and be OK with it. As Karen Taylor Good* sings, "You don't always get what you want; you get what you need."

In my practice, I often take clients who are facing heavy-duty law suits and court cases and need all the help they can get. I spend a lot of time coaching them and working through the Radical Forgiveness process using all the different Tipping Method tools.

The goal is to fine tune their energy field to the point where they have little or no enmity left towards the other party and their lawyers, and to where they are able to feel love for them at least some of the time. (Bear in mind that love in this sense means accepting them as divine beings and recognizing that they are being guided to do what they are doing just like the rest of us. It still doesn't mean we have to like them as human beings.)

When they enter the court room or engage in settlement negotiations around a table, I want them to be in a state of high vibration, emanating the energy of love and totally surrendered to the outcome. After that, it's up to Spirit.

Karen Taylor-Good is a professional singer/songwriter who has worked with us many times and whose songs are a perfect fit for us.

RESOURCES FOR THIS APPLICATION:
(Details in the Resources Section at the back of this
book and at www.radicalforgiveness.com.)

Book: *Radical Forgiveness*

Worksheets:
Radical Forgiveness Worksheet
Radical Self-forgiveness/Self-Acceptance Worksheet
Radical Manifestation Worksheet
Radical Transformation Worksheet

Audio: *Songs by Karen Taylor-Good*

25 Practical Uses for Radical Forgiveness:
Solving the Problems and Challenges of
Everyday Life in a New Way

PART THREE

Applications for Better Relationships

Preamble:

What are Relationships for Anyway?

Before launching into the practical aspects of how to use Radical Forgiveness to influence how we create, improve or wind up our relationships, I think it will be helpful if I give a brief explanation of the underlying spiritual purpose of relationships in order to set the context for the applications that follow.

Seen from the perspective of the 'Soul's Journey' model I outlined at the beginning of this book, the purpose of relationships is met in two ways. Each one occurs in a different phase of our life and under a totally different set of assumptions in each case. There is also a transitional phase, which we have referred to as the Awakening, and it is during this time that we are likely to transition from one type of relationship to another.

Relationship based on domination, control, inequality, etc., designed to create the experience of pain and separation	A W A K E N I N G	Relationship based on mutual love and respect freedom and equality, while seeing the divinity in the other and expanding into Love
Abuse, Domination, Control, Exploitation **An "I-It Orientiation**		Giving and receiving support **An "I-Thou" Orientation**

Fig. 9: *The Transition*

As you now know, during the first phase, we are here on the earth plane to experience the opposite of Oneness in order to understand what Oneness really is. It is during this first phase that we want to learn what separation is all about. For that reason, then, we come together in relationship to provide opportunities to feel the pain of separation in a wide variety of forms, such as abandonment, rejection, discrimination, abuse, violence, and so on.

Relationships provide the contexts in which such experiences can occur. As you know, this phase is known as the Spiritual Amnesia Phase. Having incarnated, we forget everything we know about where we came from, what our assignments are, what soul agreements we made and how much pain of separation we requested. This is necessary because if we knew what the agreement was, we would not enter into the dramas and situations necessary to fulfill our agreements. We would not even be aware that the purpose of relationships in this first phase is to create the pain of separation. We imagine that it's about being happy, and that's the assumption on which we proceed. It's a perfect setup.

We remain in this unconscious state until we have reached our target for the amount of karmic points we agreed to have. (Karmic points are a way of giving units of measurement for how much pain is involved.)

When that moment is reached, people awaken, usually at around the halfway point in their lives, typically between ages 45 and 65. The process of Awakening might take 2-5 years to fully develop, but once this has happened and we have properly entered the Awakening phase of our lives, the purpose of relationship shifts 180 degrees. It then becomes a matter of supporting each other in staying awake, feeling connected, being of service and Expanding into Love.

This is when we find out about Radical Forgiveness. We will have ignored it completely while in the first phase, since it only would have gotten in the way. But once we have awakened, we begin to use it to go back in time and clean out all the old energy tied up in the stories of pain and separation we created in the Spiritual Amnesia Phase. It is of no use to us now and will become toxic it remains there.

It is essential that we do this work so we can bring into present time all the energy we have invested into holding onto those stories, beliefs and assumptions based in victim consciousness. Without this work, our vibration won't improve much because the energy remains stuck in the body and keeps it down.

This can take a lot of work, and without the tools of Radical Forgiveness it would be almost impossible to achieve. There are so many stories, so much pain endured, and so many wrong assumptions to overcome, so many people to forgive, and so many circumstances to reconfigure in our minds before we are able to see the perfection in them.

When it comes to going back and undoing the projections, though, the difficulty is that the shadow material we were subconsciously projecting was, and still is, buried in the subconscious. We don't know it's there. It's the same with some of our wounds.

So we still need other people to mirror for us those parts of ourselves we have denied, repressed and projected. For that

129

reason, relationships are essential to this process even while we are in the Awakening phase.

Fig. 10: *"If you Spot it, You got it."*

Without others still pushing our buttons, we would never know what remains to be healed. The difference is that now we realize the true purpose of relationship, and we do it for each other with awareness, humor, respect and love.

There is also likely to be a need to go back one, two or even more generations to heal the patterns of pain and suffering created in the distant past. These patterns keep on getting repeated from generation to generation, even though their original purposes have expired.

One example of generational pain is that which comes from the energy pattern of slavery. There are many such examples that go way back in time. While these had spiritual purpose for those particular groups – both the victims and the perpetrators

– at some time in their spiritual evolution, they no longer serve them today and need to be transformed through Radical Forgiveness.

People often come to our workshops with pain that turns out to be not really their own but their parent's or grandparent's pain that they have taken on and made their own. I take the opportunity to admonish them for taking away someone else's pain, robbing them of their spiritual growth. Now, of course, I understand why a young person would see their mother in pain and would volunteer to carry it for her until she was strong enough to carry it herself. But they forget to give it back, become attached to it and make it their own. And of course, this inevitably shows up in that young person's adult relationships.

It takes a lot of commitment to do this clean-up work, but it can be done over time. No need to rush it. Doing the work with others of like mind helps a great deal, so it's a good idea to do a Radical Forgiveness workshop from time to time, and/ or take one of our online programs to focus on a particular story that is not easy to release.

More often than not, it's about your parents. It nearly always comes back to one or both of them. The reason is that, in order to fulfill our goal of creating the number of karmic points we signed up for, we are likely to have chosen parents who would provide a series of hurts and woundings that we could leverage by repeating them in all our subsequent relationships.

If we had agreed to take on a lot of spiritual growth during this one lifetime, we would have chosen at least one of the parents to be something of a tyrant, a drunkard perhaps, maybe even an abuser. Then we would marry someone with much the same tendencies... probably more than once.

It comes as quite a surprise to a lot of people when it is pointed out to them that they have a pattern of repeating the same kind of separation event over and over again, with very similar people showing up to support them. You might see if you are in a repeating pattern by taking this brief Relationship Survey:

1. Reviewing your romantic relationships from an early age, see if any of the following apply to you:

> a) My relationships all last approximately the same length of time before declining: **Y/N**
>
> b) My spouse is not unlike my parent of the same sex: **Y/N**
>
> c) I seem to attract the same kind of person to be in relationship with each time: **Y/N**
>
> d) My partners seem to be wonderful for the first 6 months or so and then turn abusive: **Y/N**
>
> e) I seem to be unable to sustain a long-term relationship: **Y/N**
>
> f) I always end up getting hurt: **Y/N**
>
> g) I am unable to attract a partner: **Y/N**

If you answered Yes to any of these questions, you will have had an underlying energetic pattern that was causing you to keep recreating these circumstances as self-created opportunities to heal something deep within you – but not until the time is right to do so *(i.e., when you have awakened to the truth and have begun to remember who you are and what you came here to do).* Radical Forgiveness will help you dissolve the energetic pattern, whether or not you know what the underlying issue is or was. The tools provided and/ or the RF processes you experience will automatically free you from these patterns.

2. Have any of the following repeatedly shown up in many of your relationships?

- Betrayal
- Abandonment
- Severe Disrespect
- Being Discounted and Ignored
- Lies and Withholding of Information
- Deceit and Secrets
- Infidelity
- Control and Manipulation
- Physical Abuse
- Emotional and Mental Abuse
- Sexual Abuse
- Severe Rejection
- Punishment
- Other

If so, this is a reflection of a core-negative belief that you deserve to be treated in this way. Someone planted that idea in your mind at some time. More than likely it was your parents who planted it, along with other things that created separation.

133

If it is the case that most, if not all, your separation events originated with your parents, you have a choice: You can either do the forgiveness work on your parents directly, or choose the person who, in a later event, did much the same things to you. *It makes no difference because all those leveraged events are held together by the same energy field.* Collapse the one energy field and you neutralize them all. My advice is to choose the relationship where you have the most emotional energy.

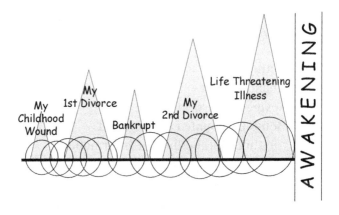

Fig. 11: *Energy Links Them All*

Having said that, I still believe it is worth doing the online 21-Day Program for Forgiving Your Parents, no matter what, especially if they are still alive. It is so sweet to be able to do the forgiveness work on our parents before they die, so that the energy between us and them is clean. That way, they are much more likely to die peacefully and be able to move on quickly when they get to the other side. It also makes your grieving process much easier. Even if they are dead already, do the forgiveness work on them anyway. It helps you on this side of the veil and them on the other. (See Application #21.)

Of course, not everyone chose to have 'bad' parents as the starting point. We may have had parents who were loving and kind, but later on found one particularly 'nasty' relationship. It could also be an event that was a starting point for us, such as an accident, an illness, a bankruptcy or a severe loss of some kind.

We tend to think that relationships happen by chance. They don't. In most cases we made an agreement with a number of souls prior to our incarnation to meet up and interact in a particular way that would give us the experience of joining and separating.

There is a great deal of very persuasive anecdotal evidence to support the idea that much of what happens to us during our lifetime was preplanned and subject to a soul agreement made prior to incarnation. Past life regression hypnotherapists, mediums, psychics, channelers and the millions of reported near death experiences support this idea, as well as the notion that we are members of a soul group who tend to incarnate together to play various roles with and for each other. Once we know this, we are able to see our enemies as our soul partners.

Obviously relationships are key to how well all such agreements play out, so we should not avoid them – no matter if it hurts. Even when we are awakened and in Phase Two of our spiritual journey, things still happen in relationships that provide opportunities for learning and growing, as we try to move into a more enlightened way of loving and relating. It's how we deal with our relationships that makes the difference.

First of all, we recognize them as opportunities to heal and grow. Second, we stay present to our feelings and let them be what they are. We do the 4-Steps Process in our minds to help shift the energy. If something serious occurs, we do a Radical Forgiveness worksheet or listen to the 13 Steps audio.

The challenge in how we relate to each other, as philosopher and theologian Martin Buber (1878 – 1965) put it, is to move from what he called an "I-It" relationship, where one relates to another as an object to be possessed and dominated (my wife, my husband), to an "I-Thou" relationship. In an "I-Thou" relationship, the "I" does not objectify the other as an "It," but instead becomes aware of having an authentic relationship with him or her. This creates a relationship based on mutual respect, as opposed to the unspoken control and domination typically negotiated in marriages during the first phase.

When we move from the I-It form of love into the I-Thou form, relating becomes about responding in the moment to the other person's needs and desires. Rather than limit their freedom to be who they are by demanding they conform to what we want them to be, we consciously decide how we wish to relate to each other, how we can meet our partner's needs and respect his or her boundaries. Out of this arises a deeper level of intimacy, mutual trust and true sharing.

This way of loving can be applied not just to our romantic partners or spouses, but to our children, siblings, parents and other members of our family, friends and neighbors, and even to people we meet only in passing, like the person at the checkout counter in a grocery store, for example.

It has to be said, however, that this does not happen automatically just because you have awakened. In fact, very few people manage to shift from their long established and habitual "I-It" way of relating to an "I-Thou" orientation. It takes effort to break the habit.

Nevertheless, by shifting into this new awareness of who your partner is and by practicing relating to him or her in the way of "I-Thou," you will be able to expand into a new, more loving relationship, not only with your partner, but with yourself, too.

I trust this preamble has been helpful in setting the stage for the next few topics on the practicalities of being in relationship and how Radical Forgiveness can be of use.

Application #11:

Make Peace with Your Family of Origin and Heal Generations Past

Radical Forgiveness constitutes the fast track to making peace with all the members of your family at all stages and several generations back as well.

Our experience indicates that around 90% of all issues that trouble people in their adult life have their origins in things that happened to them in childhood within the family unit, primarily at the hands of their parents. The same was true for their parents too, and for their parents, going back many generations. It is safe to assume that the family unit is the principal source of everyone's pain.

There is, in fact, recent scientific evidence to prove that emotional pain, if not released, is carried forward in the genes of each generation down the line. This means the pain that a lot of people are experiencing in their lives can have its origins from as far back as seven generations.

This fact alone should be reason enough for anyone with children, or an intention to have any, to stop that pain right now using the tools of Radical Forgiveness, so they don't pass it on to their own children and their children's children. The pain needs to stop here!

Grandparents, aunts, uncles and other members of an extended family may also have had a big influence on our lives. If we had siblings, they might have been a cause of pain, too. They all need our forgiveness if we are to be free from their toxic influence, and to allow the family itself to heal.

Families can be extremely toxic. Many are or were extremely dysfunctional, especially where alcohol was or still is a factor. Incest, beatings and abuse of all kinds are all too common in many apparently 'respectable' families.

Family secrets and family taboos are extremely unhealthy as well. They fester in the dark recesses of the collective mind of the whole family and wreak havoc among the individual members.

George W. Bush was the victim of such a family taboo. When his severely handicapped younger sister died at an early age, it became taboo for her name to be mentioned. George had been very attached to her and had been the one who had taken care of her until the moment she died. It hurt him terribly that he had to shut her out of any and all conversation with his parents and his siblings. It was all the more painful that there was a large picture of her hanging in the dining room for him to see while he was eating. He took to drinking and acting out irresponsibly for many years before becoming President. What effect it had on his actual presidency, we will never know, but it is known that he carries that pain in his heart to this day.

However, referring back to what I said in the Preamble, I do believe we chose our parents and all our family members before we incarnated. We made agreements with them to give us the experiences of separation we wished to experience in order to get them early. That way we could leverage them many times over with other people during the first phase of our lives when we were out to accumulate the number of karmic units we agreed get before awakening. Who better than our parents to do this for us?

I think it is highly likely, too, that our siblings were part of our 'soul group,' and that we all have had many lifetimes together, playing different roles for each other in a whole string of lifetimes. Our grandparents, too, might have been in that same soul group, as might have been our own children. We might have been together for many lifetimes as well. Who knows?

We have found over the years that entertaining the 'soul contracts idea' as a possibility will make forgiving your family members a whole lot easier. If you were to rely on traditional forgiveness, I doubt it would ever happen. Radical Forgiveness constitutes the fast track to making peace with all the members of your family at all stages, and back several generations as well.

At the human level, I don't suppose your parents were much different from most. They did the best they could and made what seemed to be a lot of very human mistakes along the way. In doing so, they either intentionally or unintentionally acted in ways that wounded you.

The wounds you suffered at that time as a child might not seem so bad now, and you may even have forgotten about them. But the wound really hurt at that time, and might have gone very deep, only to be acted out in later life as a repeating pattern.

In fact, even after you have awakened, these wounds may even now continue to determine aspects of your life in a variety of ways. They may have become the touchstones for your sense of who you are and your own self-worth. They may still decree how successful you will become. They may still affect every aspect of your life and all your relationships, oftentimes causing you to be needy, co-dependent, demanding, or passive.

Even though they served you well in giving you the experience of separation, you need to become aware of these habits of mind so they don't keep you trapped forever. You don't need them anymore.

No matter how badly hurt you were by one or both parents, the Radical Forgiveness process will help you release the repressed anger, heal the pain, and release any core negative beliefs you formed about yourself, like "I will never be enough," "I'm unlovable," "I have to be perfect in order to be loved," and so on.

If you can see how such beliefs may have gotten in the way of having good relationships, and perhaps even financial success and joy in your life, I hope you can also see how forgiving your parents, not to mention your grandparents, aunts and uncles for causing you to have those beliefs, could be the key to freeing you from all your self-imposed limitations.

As far as needing to forgive siblings is concerned, you will come to realize that your rivalries and fights were agreed upon before coming onto the earth plane and were serving a spiritual purpose. At the same time, however, we have to acknowledge that they were indeed often quite painful. Not

142

only did they cause a lot of suffering in each other, but for everyone else in the family as well.

[Just to be clear, I am using the word sibling here as a generic term to include brothers, sisters, half-brothers, half-sisters, step-siblings, adopted siblings and any other person who is broadly of the same generation as you and considered to be part of your family of origin.]

Upsets between siblings seldom exist in isolation from the family, so any upset with a sibling may be far from simple. When you look at it, the actual grievance may not actually be about your brother or sister at all. Again, it may go all the way back to childhood. Your parents may have treated you differently and set you up for jealousy, competition, rivalry and need for approval. A parent exhibiting unfair or extreme favoritism towards your brother or sister can lead you to hate him or her, even though it was not their fault.

Fortunately though, doing the Radical Forgiveness process on your sibling could have the effect of automatically healing all these underlying family issues. You don't even need to know what the underlying issues are; it happens automatically. You will just notice the change.

We saw earlier that maintaining a grudge or grievance against anyone, for any length of time, no matter who it is, can only be bad for your health and wellbeing. But because it's all in the family, the pain involved and the negative effects on your overall health and wellbeing are magnified many times over. The ties are too strong for it not to matter. And that's why it cannot be left to fester only to get handed on to the next generation, which it will be if not dissolved.

143

Since few people today have only one spouse, serial marriage and blended families are the norm, and this has become an absolute minefield in which relationships between siblings become soured, with each of them becoming embittered and full of resentment towards each other. This inevitably gets handed down to the next generation and so it goes on. This is another good reason why we should clear the energy with our siblings before our own children take it on as their own pain.

Conflicts that can fester between siblings can range from the sexual molestation of a younger sibling by an older one to the issue of how their elderly parents should be cared for. Finally, conflict can arise as they fight over how the estate is divided upon their parents' death.

There are millions of people who have never spoken to their brothers or sisters again on account of what happened with the money and other items of value when their parents died, and how the wills, property, and even keepsakes and family heirlooms were handled.

It's very sad. But again, it often goes right back to childhood – the competition and rivalry and favoritism. The men often get much more of the money than the women. I remember one case where a rich businessman left three million dollars to his two sons, but not one penny to his daughter. She had spent many years of her life looking after him, while the two brothers did nothing for him. Her father's reasoning: She was a woman and didn't need it. She would just get married. Unfortunately, this kind of thing still happens today.

We have a full array of tools and processes to use on all your family members in order to transform all the toxic energy into Love, including a Releasing Toxic Secrets Program and a number of online programs and worksheets for forgiving parents, siblings and even your own children. (See Application #12.)

You must use these tools in order to reap the benefits yourself. To do Radical Forgiveness is to release all the stored negative energy held in your body, mind and spirit so you can restore yourself to a feeling of peace and harmony. It is not the goal of Radical Forgiveness that you end up liking your family members any more than before, especially if you have spent many years disliking them.

Having said that though, when you do RF on a family member with whom there once was love and acceptance, you may find that the love is restored. Furthermore, you may be pleasantly surprised at how things change between you and all members of your family. Things that may have kept you apart for years are likely to be resolved. That's because, when you do this work yourself, for yourself, the healing goes out to the whole family.

You will recall that in Application #5, we showed how when one person in an energetic field (morphogenetic field) changes their energy, everyone else is affected. Well, a family is a morphogenetic field also, so when you do the work on yourself and your energy changes, the whole family is likely to change too. It's the law of resonance in operation. In Application #18, we show how this works in a company. When one employee shifts his or her energy, it can change everything. So as you do the work, observe what happens with the family. Note the changes, but don't say anything. You'll just smile.

RESOURCES FOR THIS APPLICATION:
(Details in the Resources Section at the
back of this book and at
www. radicalforgiveness.com.)

Worksheet: *Radical Forgiveness* Worksheet

Online Programs:
*Radical Self-Forgiveness/Self-Acceptance/Releasing
Secrets
"Breaking Free." A 21-Day Program for Forgiving
Your Parents
"Family Matters." A 21-Day Program for Forgiving
Your Siblings
"Great Expectations." A 21-Day Program for
Forgiving Your Kids*

Audio: *Radical Self-Forgiveness Practices (CD)*

Application #12:

How to Survive the Slings and Arrows of Parenting

We speak of the joy of parenting, but seldom do we discuss the pain and anguish that kids from early childhood to late adult stages visit on their parents in sometimes cruel and heartless ways.

I'm including parenting as one of the 25 practical uses for Radical Forgiveness, because there is no doubt about it; kids can drive you crazy at every stage of their development. There's not much let-up when they become adults either.

You definitely need something to help you deal with the ever-changing landscape of parent/child relationships, from coping with preschooler tantrums and adolescent angst, all the way to the point where the roles get reversed and you become the child and they become the parent. Along the way there are going to be many opportunities to practice Radical Forgiveness.

Another reason to include it is that parenting is not much discussed, in spite of the fact most of us become parents. We speak of the joy of parenting, but there's little recognition of the stress and strain we experience at every stage of the parenting process. Even less discussed is the pain and anguish that children in their early and late adult stages visit on their parents in sometimes cruel and heartless ways.

In recognition that parenting can be a lifetime project, I will briefly outline each stage and the challenges that accompany them for which Radical Forgiveness may provide some respite if not solve the problem entirely. I'll ignore the baby stage, which certainly has its challenges, but to blame the baby for them is seldom appropriate. But the others are:

1. Preschool to Pre-Adolescence
2. The Early Teens   3. The Late Teens

4. The Young Adult Child   6. The Elderly Adult Child
5. The Mature Adult Child

Few parents would say they regret having had their children. In fact, most say it has given meaning and purpose to their lives. But there are times when our children behave in ways that test our patience, tolerance and understanding to the very limits, sometimes to the point where we are at a loss to know how to handle them in the right way.

Adding to the normal parenting challenges of the past, today there is a huge generation gap between parents and their children who are steeped in the Information Age. Remember, the Internet as we know it did not even exist until the mid-90's, and at the turn of this century only 31% of people in the developed world had access to it; but since then use has skyrocketed to where it is ubiquitous. Most people younger than 20 barely remember a world without it. While their parents may also feel they don't remember what it was like before they had computers, tablets, and cell phones, the reality is that children today learn, process information, and communicate very differently from their parents. This makes even the elementary years much more challenging than they have been for past generations, with "electronics usage" a common element of conflict in many households.

Using a Radical Forgiveness Worksheet to shift the energy around a particular situation or form of behavior can be very helpful. It can be especially helpful during the teenage years, when we want to shift the energy around a challenging situation. I'm referring to the typical kind of thing that most kids create to test us from time to time. It doesn't have to be anything too serious; even average adolescent behavior is worthy of our taking some time out to process it energetically.

Now, of course, we pretty much expect teenagers to give us problems, since we know it is all part of growing up. However, if a teenager is acting out in extreme ways, like taking drugs, body piercing, being promiscuous, getting pregnant, committing crimes, acting out anger, rejecting discipline and going against all your values and morals, then again Radical Forgiveness will help enormously. It might stop you from going prematurely grey!

149

Self-esteem is a big issue with kids at this age, and many of them are depressed. This leads to all sorts of aberrant behavior, like cutting and damaging themselves in other ways. They may even make attempts at suicide, hopefully all unsuccessful, but not always.

What about adult children? Another expectation we have when we start a family is that our role as parents will end when the kids leave home and get married, and that their behavior or the decisions they make as adults will cease to be our concern. Wrong! There can be plenty of potential upset, disappointments and worries for you during this phase as well.

Who they marry, whether or not they have children, whether they get divorced, have abortions, experience bankruptcies, commit crimes, etc., are all causes for intense worry and anxiety for parents of adults. What if you don't get on with the partner – assuming there is one still around – or they make a career choice you think is a poor one? If they move a long way away or even emigrate, that can feel very much like abandonment, especially if there are grandchildren present or expected in the future.

If anything, the ability of children to cause you pain and anguish increases with age – both theirs and yours. In many cases, the need for forgiveness is actually increased, not decreased.

In early middle age (the mature adult child), often marriage breakups begin to occur and the fighting starts within their family. What parent wouldn't be deeply concerned to see a child's marriage disintegrating, especially if children are involved? Who wouldn't automatically have strong opinions and judgments about the situation? Who wouldn't want to apportion blame, especially towards the child's partner? What parent wouldn't have strong feelings to deal with that would keep them up at night? Who wouldn't want something to help ease the pain? And I don't mean drugs!

Besides using the RF tools on your own child, you can use them to forgive the spouse or partner as well. The only caveat I make about that is that you can only do it for yourself, not on behalf of your child. You cannot do forgiveness for other people, only for yourself. So, you would blame your child's spouse or partner for upsetting you, not your child. It would help you tremendously, though, to move through the pain and anguish if you were to forgive both.

And remember Application #11? Most of us parented our children in our pre-Awakened state, which means we probably did at least a few things we regret. It may be that you can make connections between the pain your adult child is suffering now with pain you inflicted on them when they were young. Anyone regretting their past parenting actions should grab a Radical Self-Forgiveness Worksheet and get started now.

Early middle age is also the time when addictions that may have been developing for years and up to now kept well hidden start to take a heavy toll. Having an addiction to things like gambling, alcohol, sex, drugs, food, etc., can be devastating, not only to their own lives but to those around them, including you.

The only thing you can do that will help you, and your child too at an energetic level, is to forgive him or her and send unconditional love and support out to them through doing this work for yourself, and sharing these tools with them if you can. It is the most loving and supportive thing you can do for someone who is in the grip of an addiction. (See Application #7.)

The most hurtful thing I see people – mostly mothers – come to my workshops suffering from is the adult child who suddenly cuts off all communication. The parent had a great connection with their son or daughter up to a certain moment in time, and then the adult child withdraws completely, often for no apparent reason; or if there is a reason, they won't say what it is.

Worse yet, they deny access to the grandchildren and block any attempt on the part of the mother to communicate with them. This causes a great deal of distress, and I would venture to say that if this happens to a parent, despite all the other pain and anguish involved in the process of raising kids, there is nothing that compares. It is the worst.

Fathers can come in for some rough justice, too, especially if they are falsely accused by their child of sexual abuse in the early years. This often happens after the child has seen a hypnotherapist and had supposed flashbacks. Not that the mother escapes the child's wrath, for she gets blamed for not protecting him or her. This can cause terrible pain and hurt.

If it truly is a false accusation, the most self-supporting thing you can do for yourself, and the most loving thing you can do for your child, is to do the Radical Forgiveness work and collapse the energy pattern in you that you might have passed through to your child. You may not know what that energy pattern is, or what caused it, but Radical Forgiveness and Radical Self-Forgiveness will take care of it automatically. I cannot explain how it will, but believe me, I know from many years of experience that it does.

Once our dear son or daughter hits 50, a subtle shift starts to occur. A sort of role reversal begins to take place, where he or she takes on the role of caretaker or parent and begins to treat you as the child. This is quite natural, of course, since you will inevitably be in your senior years now, or soon will be, perhaps not as strong or fit as you once were, and in need of some care and support from your children.

Most children do step up to the plate and do their very best to support their elderly parents, and I hope this is or will be the case with you. But sadly, it is not unusual for this role reversal to result in various forms of abuse perpetrated by the child on the parent, including such things as mental cruelty, theft, degrading treatment, manipulation of wills, and more or less total abandonment once deposited in a nursing home, to name but a few.

Abuse of the elderly is an epidemic. The U.S. Department of Health and Human Services' National Center on Elder Abuse* reports at least one in ten seniors have experienced abuse, not including financial abuse. 90% of the perpetrators are family members.[2]

Of course, your child may not be abusing you in this way at all, but there may be other things, even quite small things, that your adult child is doing that annoy you, or that you have

153

judgments about. If you were to do Radical Forgiveness around it, these would suddenly cease to be a problem for you. They simply wouldn't bother you anymore, and the chances are your child would stop doing it. Wouldn't that be nice?

What I am saying is that there are countless situations in each stage of a child's life that call for a method that enable parents to work through them so that their peace and harmony are restored.

If you are suffering right now, then it's your peace, joy and harmony we are talking about being restored. Not the child's but yours and yours alone. Forgiveness is something you do for yourself, not the other person. You're the one who needs the kind of help Radical Forgiveness provides.

You can do lots of worksheets, for sure, and they will help, but the online *21-Day Program for Forgiving Your Kids* is really the one to use. It will make a difference, not only in how you feel about it all, but possibly in how your son or daughter behaves in the future.

When you release your energy around the situation, theirs may shift too and your relationship will improve immeasurably.

Once you purchase the program, it's yours forever, so you can use it over and over as time goes on and you move through all the phases of parenting.

RESOURCES FOR THIS APPLICATION:
(Details in the Resources Section at the
the back of this book and at
www.radicalforgiveness.com.)

Worksheets: *Radical Forgiveness Worksheet*

Online Program: *"Great Expectations,"* *A 21-Day
Program for Forgiving Your Kids*

Application #13:

Revive a Failing Relationship - *Make It or Break It!*

I'm not saying it is easy to forgive infidelity, but when you have a sense that there is more to it than meets the eye, you stop relating to it as a victim and begin to take it less personally.

It's not at all unusual for one's relationship to be in crisis or failure mode at the moment of our awakening. In fact, the pain involved in such a situation may be the very thing that created the awakening – the final straw, so to speak. After all, it usually takes a break*DOWN* of some sort, whether it be a marriage crisis, illness, accident, bankruptcy or something like that, to create the break*THROUGH*.

If this is the case, assuming you haven't already separated, the question becomes: Is the relationship worth saving, or has the purpose for it been served? Is it now time to move on to pastures new?

In the pre-awakening phase, the answers to these questions would have been a more straightforward decision. It's much more tricky now you know the purpose for the relationship. The purpose before was to create separation; the purpose now is to expand into Love. That puts a whole different complexion on the issue.

There was a book that came out in the 60's by Susan Gettleman and Janet Markowitz called, *The Courage to Divorce*. It gave people 'permission' to make that choice if that's what they wanted. Given that freedom, people tended to jump out of a marriage as soon as things got a little difficult. But they missed the opportunity to stay in the relationship and grow through the pain. Once they bailed, they then had to find someone else with whom to finish off what they had started with the first partner. So began serial marriages.

To help people who have awakened and are looking for some direction on how to handle a failing relationship and whether to go or to stay, there ought to be another book entitled, "The Courage NOT to Divorce." Such a book would speak to the above dilemma, and would at least suggest that people should examine the nature of the options before them.

The decision whether to go or stay is more difficult if you make the assessment that your partner has not yet gone through the awakening. If he or she is not of the same mind as you with regard to the revised purpose of the relationship and does not wish to change, it can be much more challenging. This might be a fruitful conversation to explore with your partner. Remember, though, that even if there is little alignment of spiritual values, this need not be the deal breaker.

Assuming he or she is not downright abusive, it may, in fact, offer you a greater opportunity to grow stronger spiritually. That's because Expanding into Love is about increasing your own *capacity* to love. That means being able to accept people the way they are and seeing the divinity in them no matter what. Any relationship offers the opportunity to learn how to achieve this, no matter how good or bad it is.

158

The next step after that is to make a really honest evaluation of the relationship as it is now. This will help you to decide what to do next – make it or break it.

The next application focuses on the process of reconciliation, and you will find a worksheet designed to evaluate a relationship. You might find this helpful in evaluating yours to help you decide if you want to stay or leave. It will help you evaluate all facets of the relationship, such as how much love is left in the partnership and how it has changed in nature. You may want to look at whether you still have similar values, respect for each other and enough tolerance to make it okay to be together, or not. It asks you to look at your reasons for marrying in the first place, what you expected, in what ways those expectations were not met, and so on. Also covered are the nature of your commitment and the boundaries you agreed to, explicitly and implicitly. Lastly, what would be your conditions for staying in the relationship?

In the last analysis, though, whether or not you stay or go is not really your decision, or shall I say not your ego's decision. Only your Higher Self knows what Spirit has in store for you in the future.

And how would you know what might follow if you left? One of the distinct advantages of being awake and in alignment with the new paradigm is that we don't have to know these things. Even trying to figure them out is a waste of time. If we trust and surrender to the process, and stay alive to guidance from our Spiritual Intelligence, we will be shown what to do. And if we seem to make a mistake, that will be perfect, too.

159

So the thing to do is trust the process and surrender to Spirit. You do this by doing the Radical Forgiveness worksheets on your partner and whoever else is involved in order to maintain as high a vibration as possible. You also do Radical Self-Forgiveness and Self-Acceptance worksheets on yourself so you don't lose your self-worth by going into blame and shame. (See Application #15.) Another important tool to employ under these circumstances is the Radical Acceptance Worksheet. This will enable you to begin to accept your partner the way he or she is. (See Application #16.)

But now let's take this to the next level and look at how the process of healing our shadow often plays a crucial role in causing the breakup of a marriage or long-term relationship. If you can understand how this works, it will become easier for you to forgive your partner for whatever he/she has done to cause a breakdown in the marriage. Nine times out of ten, it is infidelity.

The shadow, you will recall, is that part of us we are ashamed of and don't want to own. It's the part of us we hate so much that we push it deep down into our subconscious and unconscious minds, and we just hope against hope it will never ever see the light of day again. It is shame-based material created as a result of a childhood wound or trauma, and it's the root of our self-hatred. Better that we repress it and pretend it's not there, hiding it even from ourselves.

To describe it in energy terms, I combined two words, human and energy, to coin the word "humenergy." I like this word because it shows that the shadow material is not inactive – quite the contrary, in fact. Even though it is deeply repressed and out of our conscious awareness, it is active energy nevertheless. Like an internal gyroscope, humenergy is constantly driving and directing our lives from deep within the unconscious mind.

I coined the word initially as a way to explain to corporate clients how this healing process operates in the workplace, benefitting the employee but very damaging to the business. (This is developed fully in Applications #18 and #19.)

I defined humenergy for them as *"the subtle and largely unconscious material that every individual brings to work and acts out – almost always to the detriment to the organization and/or their own career – as a way to heal the original wound that caused it to be repressed in the first place."*

But substitute for 'brings to work' the words 'brings to a marriage' and you will begin to understand how humenergy can destroy a relationship.

The above statement is about the natural urge in all of us to bring our unconscious, negatively charged humenergy to the surface in order to be dissolved or healed. This urge comes from our drive to become whole again. (Ironically, it becomes even more intense after we have awakened, which makes it all the more important we see the purpose in it and do not take it so personally.)

Because we are so incredibly resistant to looking at our own shadow, our Spiritual Intelligence has to set up situations that enable us to act out the original wound in a symbolic way. The workplace is an ideal place to act out these dramas, and so is one's marriage. In each case one has made commitments which cannot easily be disregarded, ensuring a high degree of drama sufficient to break down the resistance. The two are often combined, especially where infidelity is concerned.

Such dynamics are often displayed by celebrities or people in positions of power. Not that they are any different in this regard to other people, but with them it becomes exposed and talked about. The case of Tiger Woods, the golfer who destroyed his marriage through several affairs with other women, is a good example. No one could understand why a person like him, at the very top of his game, would take such a risk with his marriage and his career, especially given how rich he was and how beautiful his wife was.

But that's us trying to make sense of it by using mental logic. Our ego always wants to know why and be able to figure it out. However, if we look at it from a more spiritual point of view, we can entertain at least a plausible explanation. We know, for instance, that his father put pressure on him very early in life to become a golfer - the best golfer ever, in fact. Everything else was subservient to that. But suppose that was not his soul's mission? What part of himself did he repress in order to please his father? Was he acting out his frustration in order to heal it? Was there something else he needed to heal by acting so irresponsibly? We don't know.

The tennis star Andre Agassi, in his recently released autobiography, reveals how much his father pushed him from the age of 7 to be the top player in the world, and how much Andre hated the game and all that it entailed because of it. He shows how it led him to act out with drugs and sex in the most extraordinary and strange ways. He got through it and woke up, thank goodness, in no small way due to having met and married Steffi Graff, I believe. The chances are that Tiger had a lot of anger towards his father too, so it may have been a similar situation.

I happen to know, firsthand, someone who is quite famous and highly respected in his professional field. No one would ever imagine he'd be the kind of guy to regularly visit prostitutes, but he did. And it seemed that he could not stop doing it, even though the discovery of it would ruin his reputation and lucrative business overnight.

I worked with him and found a deeply repressed memory of his mother playing with him while in the bath as a small child, which had given him erections. It was obvious that he was subconsciously acting out his repressed sexual attraction to his mother – the Oedipus complex – by finding women who were willing to be in a dominant role during sex. He was, in effect replaying the scene. Fortunately, up until that moment,

163

he had picked women who would remain discrete, so it had not escalated into a disastrous situation like it had with Tiger Woods, but it was teetering on a knife-edge, nevertheless.

Once having discovered what needed to be healed, I had him do a lot of anger work around his mother for sexually abusing him as a baby. Then I started leading him towards the idea, central to Radical Forgiveness of course, that his soul had chosen this experience and it was all part of his soul's divine plan. At the human level, we were able to see how what his mother had done to him had actually led him to fulfill his mission to become the kind of professional he was. That enabled him to forgive her, in the traditional sense. But it was only when he really got it that his soul had asked to have that experience for reasons known only to it, that he truly forgave her at a very deep level – Radical Forgiveness. After that, he slowly let go of his need to see prostitutes.

He found me by attending one of my one-day workshops. He realized the danger he was in, and saw that Radical Forgiveness might help him before disaster struck. He very wisely hired me to help him find what needed to be healed. But unfortunately, most don't because they don't understand what is happening. Neither do their partners. The only one who perhaps might have done so is Hillary Clinton. She was hurt, I'm sure, but she was able to transcend it and move on. In spite of Bill's public humiliation and shameful persecution by the hypocrites in the Republican Party, many of whom were subsequently found out to be doing much the same thing, the two of them still seem to have a marriage that works. They are a good model for how to revive a failing marriage.

164

We don't know why people sabotage themselves like this because we are not privy to their divine plan any more that we are to our own, but celebrities do seem bent on taking it to the point where they get exposed and subsequently shamed. Perhaps they do it in order to get back in touch with the original shame that lay behind their need to act it out, but with a subconscious intention to heal it once and for all.

These people are not perverts or weirdoes; they are just human beings with wounds that are coming up for healing. Their Higher Selves don't understand and don't care that doing this healing work is bad for their career or the institution they work for. All the Higher Self cares about is that the time has come to heal that humenergy so that they can become a whole human being again.

Here's the twist in all this, though. First of all, it doesn't just happen to famous people. It happens to everyone to some degree or another. We all have humenergy deep down that wants to come up for healing, and we can rest assured that it will – one day.

The trick, then, is to do what my professional client did. Recognize the symptoms before they become too obvious to everyone else, realize that it is unconscious humenergy coming up for healing, and take steps to heal it before it does irreparable damage. In other words, we need to use the tools of Radical Forgiveness the moment we begin to spot a problem. Then we can begin taking back what we have projected onto others, which is how you know what you hate in yourself - the principle being that what you find objectionable in another is what you hate in yourself. Look at how you are acting out and see if you can find what the acting out is symbolizing and do the Radical Forgiveness work around that.

Looking back with Radical Forgiveness in mind, you will begin to realize that it had to happen, and that the other people involved in the situation had to do what they did in order to support your healing process. You will see that their souls volunteered to play the roles they did for you. Just as Tiger's father, his wife, and all his girlfriends were players in his drama, the people acting out your soul's script are all part of the plan and no one made any mistakes.

It also works the other way around, of course. This is where the person we identify as the villain acts something out for someone else's healing – usually the one we perceive as being the victim. The best recent example involving someone very famous is the case of U.S. Senator John Edwards. He was found to have been involved in a very lurid affair with one of his staffers, even while running for President of the United States… and while his wife, Elizabeth, was battling with and dying from cancer. Here's an article I wrote at the time:

The John Edwards Affair
If I had known earlier what I have just learned from reading excerpts taken from Elizabeth Edwards' recently released book, I would have gone out and put money on the absolute inevitability of her husband's infidelity. I am quite certain that John Edwards had no choice in the matter. His soul did it for her healing. Let me explain.

It is clear from her own writing that ever since she was 13 years of age, Elizabeth Edwards had been carrying her mother's pain caused by the suspicion of Elizabeth's father's infidelity. Here are some of her own words:

> "At 13 I had read my mother's journals. I discovered that my mother believed my father had been unfaithful to her when I was only a baby. I will say clearly that I do not know if that is true. I only know what she suspected... that my father found other companionship while she was buried in babies. She even thought she knew where – the Willard Hotel in Washington – the place where I had my senior prom, which must have been a bitter pill for her, although I had a suitably terrible time because, unbeknownst to her, I knew what that hotel meant to her. She lived all those decades still loving him, but with something deep inside that would always be restless, even after he died. The possibility of my father's infidelity ate at my mother, I knew, but she stayed there, stayed with him and loved him, and after his stroke when he was nearly 70, she cared for him for two decades with a selflessness that is almost unimaginable.

> ***"Don't ever put me in that position," I begged John when we were newlyweds. "Leave me if you must, but do not be unfaithful."***

If ever there was a case that perfectly illustrates how unresolved pain, especially pain that is carried on behalf of someone else – usually on behalf of a parent – will find a way to become healed through re-enactment in the next generation, this is it. Elizabeth witnessed her mother being "eaten away" by the suspicion of the infidelity and it surely ate away at Elizabeth, too, all through her life.

Since cancer eats us alive, it is not too much of a stretch to implicate this trauma in the causation of her cancer. It is, after all, in the breast which is the heart chakra. In my experience in working with cancer patients, my observation is that breast cancer is often the result of a broken heart. Not only was her own heart broken in sympathy with her mother, she clearly had not forgiven her father for causing the heartbreak. Since forgiveness, or the lack thereof, is also carried in the heart chakra, along with repressed rage, I am not at all surprised she should have cancer of the breast.

This seemingly tragic story is also illustrative of how we enroll others to help us heal such deep and painful wounds. Our soul yearns for integrity and wholeness, and at some point in our journey will seek to remove anything that is preventing those qualities from arising. Sometimes this can be achieved through our own efforts, but not infrequently it requires the cooperation of another soul who will agree to act out the situation again for us. By their re-enactment, we can recognize the pain and bring it to the surface for healing through forgiveness.

This is exactly what John Edwards, quite unwittingly, of course, did for his wife. He did what Elizabeth suspected her father did so she could become acquainted with her repressed rage towards her father and come to a place of forgiveness with him. John loved her enough to sacrifice his career and humiliate himself in front of the whole world so that she might either heal her cancer, or at least die free of the pain she has carried all her life.

This is not to say that, at the human level, John Edwards is not culpable and accountable for the human act of adultery and betrayal, not to mention his stupidity. He clearly is, and he will pay the price accordingly. What I am talking about is what happened at the spiritual level, and in my opinion, it's the more meaningful explanation.

Why else would a highly educated, extremely intelligent, intensely rational person with a razor-sharp legal mind, who is perfectly able to assess the risk in any situation, running for the highest office in the land, allow himself to be drawn into a sordid little affair with that clumsy one-liner, "You're hot." This might hook a rabid sex addict, perhaps, but there's no evidence that John had that addiction. Even to a skeptic, the metaphysical explanation for John's behavior makes infinitely more sense than throwing away his career for a very risky affair with one woman.

I am absolutely convinced he (his soul) did it for Elizabeth, and furthermore, that her soul asked his soul to do it for her. It's a perfect example of the kind of soul-to-soul healing transaction that typifies what we teach in Radical Forgiveness. It provides Elizabeth with the opportunity to forgive her father and to see the "perfection" in what John did — not TO her but FOR her.

You also have to ask yourself why would anyone say to their newly wed husband, "Leave me if you must, but do not be unfaithful." That seems indicative of an obsession, I would say. She even said that it was not a premonition. "I was talking about my own history." She proves the old adage that what you focus on expands and eventually shows up. But beneath all that, her statement is, to me at least, her signal for him to actually be unfaithful at some critical moment in their lives, allowing her to heal her mother's wound and her own. And you have to admit, he sure did choose the right moment for maximum effect.

If I were advising Elizabeth, or anyone else for that matter who was clearly holding on to someone else's pain, I would recommend two courses of action.

1. Do a Radical Forgiveness worksheet on her father to release all that repressed rage and judgment towards him. Better still, do the online *"Breaking Free" 21-Day Program for Forgiving Your Parent.* She could also do the *"Moving Forward" 21-Day Program for Forgiving Your Partner* to work through her suffering from John betraying her. I would also advise her to do a Radical Forgiveness worksheet on the other woman because she was part of the plan too. Without her, it wouldn't have happened. John would be advised to do one on her for the same reason.

2. Give her mother's pain back. Regardless of whether her mother is dead or not, she can release the need to hold on to her mother's pain. Not only is it highly toxic to Elizabeth and likely to nourish her cancer, from a spiritual point of view she has no right to hold on to it. By doing so, she is preventing her mother's soul from having the learning experience she was being offered in her own lifetime. Elizabeth is, in effect, stealing her mother's karmic gold, and she should return it forthwith.

I would love to work with John and Elizabeth in my Miracles Workshop. I know it would help them move through this experience and both would come out stronger and full of love for each other. And who knows — she might come out cancer free. It's happened before.

End of Article

As we now know, Elizabeth did die. John was further shamed when it came out that he had fathered a baby with the other woman, even after vehemently denying it on TV many times. Clearly he had a lot of his own humenergy to heal as well.

So now you know what might save a failing relationship if the cause was some major betrayal like infidelity. I'm not saying it is easy to forgive things like that in the normal sense of the word, but at least once you have a sense that there is more to it than meets the eye, you stop relating to it so much as a victim, and you begin to take it less personally. See it as an opportunity to expand your capacity to love, even if divorce is inevitable. Accept the person as they are, knowing that we all are battling to heal our shadow and become whole. Be like Hillary Clinton and rise above hurt. This might be your best chance to save a failing marriage.

RESOURCES FOR THIS APPLICATION:
(Details in the Resources Section at the back of this book and
www.radicalforgiveness.com.)

Worksheets:
Radical Self-Forgiveness/Self-Acceptance Worksheet
Radical Acceptance (of another) Worksheet

Online Programs:
Radical Self-Forgiveness/Self-Acceptance/Releasing Toxic Secrets
"Breaking Free." A 21-Day Program for Forgiving Your Parents
"Moving Forward." A 21-Day Program for Forgiving Your Partner

Workshop: *'Expanding in Love.' A Weekend Workshop*

Application #14:

How to Negotiate for a Win-Win Reconciliation

Where there is inherent conflict between your partner's boundaries and your own, you will have to agree to work out a compromise you both can live with. If you cannot find a compromise, then you may have to let the relationship go.

We have learned already that the spiritual context within which we create and navigate our relationships changes once we reach the point of awakening. Instead of providing specific kinds of drama for the sake of our soul's need to experience the pain of separation, it now becomes a matter of creating opportunities to expand into Love.

Let me remind you that Expanding into Love means much more than simply increasing your romantic love for your partner, though this is nice if it occurs. As I said in the previous chapter, Expanding into Love is about increasing your *capacity* to love. That means being able to accept people the way they are and seeing the divinity in them no matter what. This is irrespective of whether there is romantic love there, or you are breaking up. Any relationship offers the opportunity to learn to achieve this no matter how good or bad it is.

In the previous chapter we discussed why spousal relationships fail and how they might be saved if we apply Radical Forgiveness to the situation. Now let's look at how we might

173

go to the next step and consciously renegotiate the relationship in the context of Radical Forgiveness. *[If you have already decided to break up, you might still do the worksheet as preparation for how you would want to negotiate any new relationship you create in the future.]*

This deserves its own application because, in all other circumstances where Radical Forgiveness is the answer to a problem, the only person doing the forgiveness work is you. In this situation, you need both parties engaged in this process. Reciprocity is definitely required, which means both parties must be willing participants.

I have designed a Radical Reconciliation Worksheet for each partner to use and this is outlined below.

The process I recommend is for the partners to do the worksheet independently without conferring. When they have completed it, they come together and share their worksheets openly and frankly, section by section. They must be willing to be brutally honest and hold nothing back. I will share a good method for doing this discussion process after I have outlined the steps of the worksheet.

>   **Part 1:** Evaluating where things stand now versus how it was at the beginning.

>   **Part 2:** Recognizing where changes might be made and what might need to be done to shift the energy.

>   **Part 3:** Coming to a reframe of the current and past situations.

Part 4: Declaring what you would want in the relationship for the future.

When you come to the fourth part, you need to really think hard about how you want the relationship to be and exactly where your boundaries lie. To be clear, it is not about imposing on the other person, making demands they can't meet, setting expectations they cannot fulfill or controlling them in any way.

We discussed this in the application outlining the purpose of relationships and how we relate to each other after we have awakened. This will be challenging for a lot of people, especially those who have been in relationship for a long time and have developed a habitual way of being based on those very behaviors which we now have to give up.

What you are doing here is simply communicating what you want and don't want in the revised relationship. It's then up to the other person to say whether they are willing and able to fulfill those requirements or not. If not, then the relationship should end, or if it is a prospective one, not even begin.

THE RADICAL RECONCILIATION
WORKSHEET

1. Venting: Before I can start the process of reconciling with you, I have to get the following off my chest about what has happened in the relationship up to now to cause the split, and trust that you will hear what I have to say and honor my experience even if it is not yours. *(Make some notes on a separate sheet, or several sheets.)*

2. How I Feel About You

On a scale of 1 - 100, where 1 = Loathing and 100 = Totally Besotted

My love for you in the beginning or at the height of our relationship was around _____

At the lowest point in our relationship it would have measured approximately _____

At this moment in time it is around _____

3. How I Think You Feel About Me

On a scale of 1 - 100, where 1 = Loathing and 100 = Totally Besotted

I think your love for me in the beginning or at the height of our relationship was _____

At the lowest point in our relationship, it felt like it was _____

At this moment in time I feel it might be around _____

4. My Thoughts Accompanying My Decision to Marry or Be in Relationship With You Were: *(Check ones that apply.)*

☐ I can never imagine life without you.

☐ I am madly in love with you.

☐ I think I am in love with you although there is still a doubt in my mind.

☐ I have doubts about us but if I love you enough, you will change and become the person I want you to be.

☐ I am very fond of you and feel we could be happy.

☐ I am unsure if I am in love you, but I am content to be with you forever.

☐ I see you more as a friend or someone who will take care of me.

☐ I am not really in love with you, but I like you well enough.

☐ I did not ever love you but felt pressured into marrying you.

☐ I hated you but I had no choice.

☐ Others:

5. My Thoughts and Feelings About Trying to Reconcile Are:

☐ I am still totally besotted and in love with you.

☐ I am still very much in love with you and want to be with you.

☐ We have so much that is good on which to build a better relationship.

☐ Even though I am not IN love with you any more, I still love you, but I am not sure I can live with you.

☐ I feel my doubts have magnified and I feel very doubtful that we can make it.

☐ I am still fond of you but I am not always happy being with you.

☐ There's too much negativity in our relationship to bear.

☐ Others: _____

6. I realize that I had expectations, demands and needs I wanted you to fulfill, and that I judged you and made a lot of assumptions I was not entitled to make. Some of these were:

☐ I expected you to love me no matter what.

☐ I always assumed we would have children together.

☐ I assumed you would make me the priority in your life.

☐ I expected you to be accepting of my ways.

☐ I judged you to be not okay the way you were and I needed you to change.

☐ I expected you to be faithful to me.

☐ I demanded you fulfill all my needs.

☐ I demanded that you put up with my mother always calling me.

☐ I assumed you would like the same things in life as I do.

☐ Others: _____

7. The demands, expectations, judgments, needs and assumptions I am totally willing to let go of now in order to reconcile are:

☐ My need and expectation that you will always love me no matter what.

☐ My assumption that we would have children together.

☐ I assumed you would make me the priority in your life.

☐ My need and expectation that you will be accepting of my ways.

☐ My judgment about you not being okay the way you are.

☐ My need for you to change.

☐ My expectation that you will always be faithful to me.

☐ My demand that you fulfill all my needs.

☐ My demand that you put up with my mother always calling me.

☐ My assumption you would like the same things in life as I do.

☐ Others: _____

8. The Things I Have to Forgive You For, Before I Can Fully Reconcile with You, Are:

1. _____

2. _____

3. _____

List more if necessary.

_____

9. Reframing the Relationship: *(Read out to each other.)*

I now realize that there has always been a spiritual purpose for our relationship and a deeper meaning for both of us in terms of our

179

own soul's journey. I recognize that we may well have made, prior to incarnating, a contract with each other to come into relationship in order to provide for each other the experiences of certain forms of separation. This is in order to support each other in coming to appreciate the true nature of Oneness, for it is only in experiencing the opposite of Oneness that we can know what it is.

I now realize that my demands, expectations and judgments made on or about you, and those you made on me, were simply opportunities for each of us to experience the pain of separation in as intense a way as possible for the most value to our souls.

As I begin now to remember the true nature of who I am and who you are, I take back all the projections I made on you as my way of trying to avoid seeing the truth. Thank you, _____, for mirroring the parts of me that I did not want to own or accept in myself, so I could heal the split within and become whole again.

Everything that I saw in you was a reflection of what I hated in myself. Some of the things you mirrored for me were:

(Examples: My lack of generosity; My need to control and manipulate others; My dishonesty and lack of integrity; My tendency to withhold love; My cruelty; My meanness; My selfishness.)

My . . .

_____

_____

_____

Thank you, _____, for mirroring those parts of me I have denied, repressed and projected onto you, and am now willing to love and accept these in myself.

180

10) Let's Make a Deal

The following will form the basis for negotiating the terms of the reconciliation. *(For b - f, I suggest you make notes on a separate sheet of paper.)*

a) I am willing to commit to doing as many Radical Forgiveness Worksheets and/or other processes as it takes to come to a place of peace about those things I listed under # 8 above.

b) The things I would like you to forgive me for are:

_____

_____

c) If we reconcile, what I would want from you now is:

_____

_____

_____

d) If we reconcile, what I am willing to give/do/be is:

_____

_____

_____

e) If we reconcile, what I am NOT willing to give/do/be is:

_____

_____

_____

f) If we reconcile, what I refuse to overlook or put up with in the future is:

_____

_____

_____

11. Dedicated Date and Time to Share Our Worksheets:
_____ and _____ agree to arrange a time to discuss the content of our worksheet without a time constraint of any kind, and in a place where we will not be disturbed or interrupted. Our phones will be off. We will use the method whereby one of us speaks for some minutes, while the other listens and does not respond other than to reflect back what was heard. The speaker then corrects their recollection of what was said and continues until it feels right to pause. The other speaks with the same privilege of being respectfully heard without interruption (an Imago technique). If either one of us feels that we would prefer to have a neutral third party facilitate the conversation under these terms, the following person(s) would be acceptable to me:

_____

How to Conduct the Discussion Session
The best way I know to have this discussion without it degenerating into an argument or creating an attack-defense cycle is to use a system developed by Harville Hendrix, author of *Getting the Love You Want,* where you each agree to follow a specific set of rules. These are:

1. You set aside an appropriate amount of time and sit opposite each other so that eye contact is possible. Partner A goes first,

182

saying what is true for him/her, while Partner B simply listens and says nothing at all. After about 5 minutes, Partner A pauses and asks Partner B to reflect back what he/she just said.

Partner B begins by saying, "What I think I heard you say was . . ." and proceeds to reflect back as accurately as possible what he/she thinks was said. He or she must not respond to what is said or say anything other than what he/she heard.

If Partner B was not accurate in his/her reflection, Partner A will say, "No, that's not quite what I said. What I said was…" Partner B reflects it again until Partner A is satisfied that he/she has been heard and acknowledged.

He or she will then continue in this way for as long as it takes to finish what he/she needs to say at that point. Partner B asks, "Are you complete?" Partner A says, "Yes."

Now it's Partner B's turn to speak while Partner A listens and reflects back. This back and forth way of communicating goes on until the conversation is complete, with each partner taking care always to retain ownership of how they are seeing the situation or feeling about it. This is achieved by always beginning with an "I" statement. "I am feeling . . ." or "The way I see it is . . ."

Never begin with a "you" statement, such as "You told me…" Rather we would say, "My recollection of the conversation was…"

This approach will help you stay out of the attack/defense cycle, but both partners must stick to the rules if it is to work.

Once the back and forth sharing has come to an end, it is best to simply say, "Thank you." Leave it at that for a moment or two before broadening it out as a discussion of what was shared. Do your best not to let it become an argument by sticking to the method of each one listening and reflecting back.

First Establish Your Boundaries

Before you begin the discussion you must really give deep consideration to what your own boundaries and limits might be at this time. They may be quite different to how they were before you shifted to the new paradigm. At that time, you might have wanted to be treated in disrespectful ways, or even abusive ways, in order to experience that pain. But you don't want to experience that anymore now, so you need to make a point of listing it as a new boundary. You must let your partner know where your limits are in terms of what you will accept and what you won't. These often rise to the level of principle and are reflective of your own sense of self as an individual and how you wish to be treated in the relationship. Some of them may even rise to the level of 'deal killers' in the sense that the relationship would not survive if they were dishonored or crossed.

Once you have both completed your lists, sit down and go through them one by one, still using the listen and reflect back approach. Where there is inherent conflict between your partner's boundaries and your own, you will have to agree to work out a compromise you both can live with. If you cannot find a compromise, then you may have to let the relationship go.

Probably the most significant boundary for most people is the issue of fidelity. At the beginning of a relationship, this is not an easy issue to discuss and is even more difficult to be honest about.

But you can at least be honest with yourself. Are you the type who is polyamorous and will find it difficult to resist the chance to indulge in a little carnal pleasure on the side? If so, you really need to give it some thought. How would you feel if your partner did the same? Are you suited to be in a marriage or serious relationship that does not allow you to be your authentic self? It could be a deal killer.

When you have been in relationship with someone for a number of years, you can be more honest, open and frank, because the likelihood is that you will be able to discuss it rationally based on how it has been for you both up to now. After all, you have a track record to go on and you know each other pretty well.

Either one of you or both may have been tested and may have failed! Is there still some forgiveness to do? How do you want it to be going forward? What would you want from your partner? What are you willing to give up in order to accommodate your partner's needs? Here are some questions and phrases that might serve as discussion points in establishing boundaries and agreements:

Commitment - What does it mean?

Commitment to what?

Intimacy - What does each of us need?

Sex - Can we be honest about this?

185

Fidelity - Are we of the same mind here?

Flirting - Where is the line to be drawn?

Freedom - From what? Freedom to do what?

Honesty - No secrets.

Openness - No hiding our feelings.

Equality - We matter equally.

Support - Taking care of each other.

Money Matters - Open and fair, equal shares, no secrets.

Responsibilities - Understood and taken seriously.

Decision Making - Joint.

What's mine? What's yours? Wills.

Roles - Voluntary and enjoyed.

Family Matters - Who comes first?

Children - Joint responsibility.

Friends - Honor and respect each other's friendships.

Religion - Respect.

Spirituality - Respect.

Personal Growth – Support.

Alcohol

Smoking

Drugs

When you have your discussion, write everything down. When you have completed your discussion and have agreed to everything, both of you read out loud to each other the following statement.

> I promise myself that I will stand by my boundary statements and the principles underlying them, and I will not sell myself out. At the same time, I am willing to look at how my partner expresses his/her boundaries and will honor those too. Where they seemed to conflict, we have made compromises that satisfy us both. We are committed to going forward with this relationship on this basis.

Signed: _____ Date: _____ _____

Application #15:

Find Love and Acceptance for Yourself, Just the Way You Are

Now is the time to come into the fullness of your divine nature as you journey on in your human body, loving yourself in your beautiful, divinely organized imperfection.

U p to now the focus has been on using Radical Forgiveness to transform what's 'out there.' In this application, we turn our attention to what's 'in here.' Here we use the process of Radical Forgiveness to come to a place of forgiveness and acceptance for ourselves.

One definition of Radical Forgiveness is the unconditional acceptance of what is, as is; because that is exactly how it is meant to be. When we apply this to ourselves we can say that Radical Self-Forgiveness is accepting the consequences of being ourselves.

We are who we are because that's exactly who we are meant to be. We are not some aberration or mistake. Neither have we made a mistake at any time in our lives. We are spiritual beings having a spiritual experience in a human body, the true purpose of which is really known only to our Higher Self and Spirit.

That said, most people would agree that finding love, forgiveness and acceptance for others is much easier than finding it for ourselves. Our own self-hatred is so deep that

189

it is very hard for us to rise above it and touch the essence of who we really are, which is Love.

Some say our self-hatred is rooted in our shame for having chosen to separate from God against His will, the original sin. I don't believe this at all. We are each part of that which we call God, and I believe we are here to experience the opposite of Love so we can further expand our consciousness of the true nature of Love.

I would venture to say that our self-hatred is the result of organized religion having drummed into us that we are sinners and in need of being saved by someone or something else. How disempowering and shaming is that? No wonder we hate ourselves.

The result of this is that we have become deeply divided within, splitting ourselves into multiple personalities or archetypes. Herein lies the problem with self-forgiveness. We are not a singular self but a whole community of selves, all of whom have different ideas of who we are and how we should show up in the world.

Included among this rabble are the inner judge, the inner lover, the inner clown, the inner parent, the inner child, the inner professor, the inner prostitute, the inner critic, the inner saboteur, just to name a few.

It's small wonder we have trouble accepting ourselves just the way we are, when we have this incredible cast of characters inside our heads all telling us conflicting things about ourselves. And they are all very noisy as well as horribly argumentative. It gets to be very confusing.

These characters are heavily influenced by people outside of ourselves who also feel they have a say in how we should be. Initially, of course, it is our parents who tell us whether we are OK or not and to whom we look for love and approval. Then it is our siblings and our peers, schoolteachers, priests and others in authority. Society itself tries to give us a rule book on how we should behave in approved ways, and then, of course, there is the influence of media.

All of these entities have a vote on how we end up feeling about ourselves and imagining who we are – without really knowing the truth. Because of them, we begin asking ourselves such questions as: "Do I fit in?" "Am I loved for who I am, or should I be different in order to get love and approval?" "Am I okay or not okay?" "Am I good enough?" "Do I have to be perfect in order to be loved?"

The two that create the most problems for us are the inner judge and the inner critic. The inner parent can be troublesome, too, so make that three. Unfortunately, these three are the noisiest members of the community, so it is often their voices we hear in our heads telling us we are not okay and that we have to be different from the way we are.

There are likely to be many things we feel guilty about and wish to forgive ourselves for, but when we appeal to these entities for forgiveness, they inevitably say, "No." Their job, as they see it, programmed as they are by religious dogma, is to deny our divinity and to make us wrong at every opportunity. This makes traditional self-forgiveness virtually impossible to achieve. It also accounts for why it is far more difficult to forgive ourselves than to forgive others.

Knowing what we know now, the solution is obvious. We do an end run around our collective human self and appeal to the one true self that recognizes the perfection of who we are, just the way we are. That is our Higher Self. It is the part of us that truly knows who we are and loves us unconditionally. As soon as we connect to this only true part of us, the rabble inside our head goes quiet. They realize they have no power left over us now. Once you have connected with your spiritual self in this manner, you will come to know yourself and accept yourself as you are.

In exactly the same way, and for precisely the same reasons, we need to make this connection through using the tools provided under the Tipping Method umbrella. In most cases it will be a Radical Self-Forgiveness/Self-Acceptance worksheet. If that isn't enough to overcome the self-loathing, you might need to use the Online Self-Forgiveness/Self-Acceptance Program.

I also recommend the Three Letter Process outlined in Application #7, which can be adapted easily to this purpose. It is a little more challenging since you have to put into the three letters more or less the same stuff as in the worksheets, but do it in your own language and style.

A tool that is very helpful in preventing you from reverting to your old habit of beating yourself up as soon as something occurs is an audio process called The 13 Steps to Radical Self-Forgiveness.

Another source of your self-hatred is the deep reservoir of toxic core-negative beliefs that you created about yourself in that first phase. Just as the human group soul created separation between male and female, so you created separation within yourself. You became split within.

One half you accepted and were willing to share with others, while the other part you came to loathe and keep hidden, not just from others, but from yourself. Carl Jung called this your shadow.

This split was formed at a very early age, and your parents were mostly instrumental in helping you create it. You learned very early on what aspects of yourself were approved of by your parents and those that were not. Those that were not were dumped into your shadow and repressed – pushed out of awareness altogether.

You then would have outwardly exhibited only those characteristics that consistently won you love and approval. Since they came mainly from your parents, they would have been culturally determined.

They formed not only your world view, but the very ideas about how you fitted into that world. This would have made them very difficult to overcome once you became aware of them and became awakened.

Nevertheless, what you can do is cast your mind back to the time before you were awake and do your best to identify, and then repudiate, the beliefs you once held to be true which now have no validity and are toxic to you. Here's an exercise extracted from my book, *Expanding into Love,* which you can use to neutralize all toxic beliefs from your energy field.

Exercise:
Go back over your life experience and try to identify what we call the 'core-negative' beliefs that lay behind each of your victim stories. Review the patterns that were revealed, plus any others that have come to mind since, and see if you can deduce a few probable beliefs you might have been acting out over the years. Then write down variations on what you think those core-negative beliefs might be. To get you started, here a few examples of typical core-negative beliefs:

I will never be enough.
It is not safe to be me.
I am always last or left out.
People always abandon me.
It is not safe to speak out.
I should have been a boy.
I'll never make it.
Life is not fair.
No matter how hard I try, it is never enough.
I am unworthy.
I'll never be successful.
It is not good to be powerful/successful/rich/outgoing.
I don't deserve _____.
I must always obey or suffer.

195

I am alone.
Other people are more important than me.
No one will love me.
I am unlovable.
No one is there for me.
I have to do it all myself.

Other: _____

The problem with trying to identify core-negative beliefs is that they tend to be unconscious. You hardly know they are there, much less what they actually say. One way to identify them is to work backwards. Look back at what keeps showing up in your life. Deduce from that what the belief must be that's creating that kind of activity.

If people consistently treat you a certain way, then you can safely assume they are energetically picking up on some belief you have about yourself. They are subconsciously treating you in alignment with that belief.

Complete your list of "likely" beliefs. Then look through them and pick out the ones that seem to have the most resonance. Write them up in a journal, and then write each one on a separate Post-it or piece of paper. Put them to one side.

You might find this next step counterintuitive and perhaps difficult to imagine, but I want you to feel love and acceptance for each one of these beliefs. Yes, I did say **"love"** them! Love them as part of who you have been up to now, and then remain open to the possibility that they have served you in some way. Love them for what they have done for you, even if you can't see it.

It's important to love them because beliefs are not just benign things that exist as connections in the brain. They cannot be turned off just like that. They exist as an integral part of your Self. In other words, if you make the beliefs 'wrong' and try to get rid of them, you are actually attacking and undermining your own Self. That's a big deal. Bringing Love to the situation by loving yourself for having the belief, and loving the belief itself prior to disavowing it, will quiet your 'Inner Judge' and make your mind more receptive to the idea that there was a purpose in having it at some time in your life, but no longer. Now you can let it go.

I'm sure you've heard of the saying, "What you resist, persists." Right? It's certainly applicable in this instance. If you resist the energy by trying to release it from a place of judgment, it will become stronger.

If you love it just the way it is, accepting it as having been a loving, supportive part of yourself you now see as no longer relevant, it will dissolve on its own. It will cease to have any vote in your reality. From this point on, it will have no power to create circumstances in your life that will support the belief.

I hope you can now see that asking, "How do I get rid of these beliefs?" is asking the wrong question. The real question is, "How can I get to a point where I can lovingly accept my belief, and love myself completely for having it, so I can let it dissolve naturally?"

Action. Take those pieces of paper on which you wrote your beliefs and, one by one, do the following.

1. Hold the belief in your left hand (which connects it to your right brain), hold it high, and then say this, with feeling:

   *"I love myself for having had the belief that . . . . and realize that this belief has served me lovingly in the past. I send love and appreciation now to this belief and the part of my ego that has felt the need to hold onto it. I feel blessed to have had it as part of my consciousness until this moment and realize now that I need to hold onto it no longer. **I, therefore, lovingly release it from my consciousness NOW.**"*

2. Now hold the belief in your right hand and say the same thing again, this time connecting with your left brain.

Repeat steps 1 and 2 three times, changing hands each time. Say the last line with gusto and plenty of voice. Put some physical energy behind it as well. Then, when you have finished doing it for that one belief, tear the paper up or burn it.

Forgive the Belief Creators

In addition to doing this exercise, it will probably be necessary for you to do Radical Forgiveness worksheets on the people who caused you to form negative beliefs about yourself. The most likely candidates are almost certainly going to be your parents. You will find that doing the work on your parents will make a huge difference in how you feel about yourself and in your relationship with them.

It is the most loving thing you can do for them and for yourself. Not that you will tell them you are doing it, of course. You just do it and observe what happens. Since nearly all the issues that arise in our adult life originate in early childhood and come right back to the parents, we have created a special 21-day online program for forgiving your parents.

All of the above notwithstanding, it has probably dawned on you by now that your self-hatred was all part of the plan. After all, what better way to experience separation than to create wars between aspects of your own self? Were not your critical parent and inner judge serving you well in keeping you out of a state of self-love until you were ready to become awakened?

Now that you have awakened, you realize that the divine purpose of the inner conflict has been served and can now be dropped. From this point on, it's all about learning to love yourself just the way you are. You are a perfect expression of the Divine. You always have been but you didn't know it until now. You are now about to come into the fullness of your divine nature as you journey on in your human body, loving yourself in your beautiful, divinely organized imperfection.

I wish I knew the author of the following ode to self-acceptance but have not been able to find it. But I like it a lot and have included it in my book, *Radical Self-Forgiveness* which, by the way is recommended reading for this subject. I am taking the liberty of including the ode here and hope that it inspires you to see how special you are. Enjoy.

199

YOU ARE SPECIAL

Created For A Special Purpose

In all the world there is nobody like you. Since the beginning of time, there has never been another person like you. Nobody has your smile. Nobody has your eyes, your nose, your hair, your hands, your voice. You are special. No one sees things just as you do. In all of time there has been no one who laughs like you, no one who cries like you. And what makes you laugh and cry, will never provoke identical laughter and tears from anybody else, ever.

You are the only one in all creation with your set of natural abilities. There will always be somebody who is better at one of the things you are good at, but no one in the Universe can reach the quality of your combination of talents, ideas, natural abilities and spiritual abilities.

Through all of eternity, no one will ever look, talk, walk, think, or do exactly like you. You are special. You are. And, as in all rarity, there is great value. Because of your great rare value, you need not attempt to imitate others. You should accept - celebrate - your differences and even those parts of yourself that you judge to be not OK.

You are special. Continue to realize it's not an accident that you are who you are. Continue to see that you were created to serve a very special purpose. Out of all the billions of applicants for that mission, only you qualified. You were the one with the best combination of what it takes. That just as surely as every snow flake that falls has a perfect design and no two designs are the same, so no two people are the same.

Ask that you continue to be guided in fulfilling your Divine Plan. Trust the process and let it unfold in perfect sequence and perfect order. Be grateful and happy.

RESOURCES FOR THIS APPLICATION:
(Details in the Resources Section at the back of this book and at www.radicalforgiveness.com.)

Books:
Radical Self-Forgiveness: The Direct Path to Radical Self-Acceptance
Expanding into Love: A Handbook for Awakening to Who You Are, Raising Your Vibration and Creating Enlightened Relationships

Worksheet: *Radical Self-Forgiveness/Self-Acceptance*

Online Programs:
Radical Self-Forgiveness/Self-Acceptance/Releasing Secrets

Audio: *13 Steps to Radical Self-Forgiveness*

Audio/Video: *Self-Forgiveness*

Package: *QEMS Q-Work Kit*

Consultation: *By appointment*

Application #16:

Find Love for the Other Guy Even If He Is a Jerk

As we realize our dislike for the person was simply our own self-loathing projected out onto him or her, we connect ever more deeply to the Love that is always there.

I've always argued that in order to forgive a person, you don't have to like them. I continue to stand by that statement, if only because it enables people to begin the forgiveness process without reservation. You cannot even begin to forgive a person you despise if there is a prior requirement that you must like them first, or even afterwards. It is not possible.

I have also said that if the person remains toxic to you once you have forgiven them, or poses a threat to your safety, you should remove yourself from that person's presence. I stand by that, too. Martyrdom is not required.

Elsewhere in this book I have cited the adage, *'What you resist, persists.'*

203

The same applies here to liking someone. Trying to overcome a dislike by willful struggle is sure to increase it.

So, as in all the processes that I teach, we have to begin where we are and accept what is. If we have a need to forgive someone, we are almost certain to have a negative opinion, if not an active dislike of them for having done something bad to us. We must begin from that point.

However, what is true in my experience is that Radical Forgiveness, while it does not demand that you like your attacker, will automatically remove the **BASIS** for your dislike. What fuels your dislike are your judgments, your expectations, your demands, your need to control, etc. Victim consciousness is the oxygen that feeds the fire of your dislike. In earlier chapters on relationships, we showed the dangers of wanting or expecting the person to be different from the way they are.

While traditional forgiveness continues to support such demands, the process of Radical Forgiveness systematically dissolves them. The result is you end up, if not actually liking the person, at least feeling different about them - neutral perhaps, with very little energy left one way or the other.

But that's not the end of it. The real goal of Radical Forgiveness is to heal the illusion of separation that exists between you and the other person and to join in Love. You might recall the story in Chapter 3 about the Little Soul making an agreement with another soul to come into his life at some point to do something to him that would give him an opportunity to experience himself as the Light. This is what this is all about.

When we do Radical Forgiveness, we are opening to the possibility that the person we dislike, even if they haven't done anything to us to actually forgive them for, is offering us the opportunity to heal the myth of separation and remind us of our own divinity. Once we recognize this is what is happening, all our judgments, demands and expectations drop away and the dislike evaporates. As we recognize the divinity in that person, we connect with the Love that is always present in any relationship.

We also experience a sense of gratitude for this person coming into our lives to help us heal the separation within by reflecting back to us what we have, up to now, found so unacceptable in ourselves. As we realize through the Radical Forgiveness process that our dislike for the person was simply our own self-loathing projected out onto him or her, and that this person is our healing angel, we connect ever more deeply to the Love that is always there.

This applies also to extreme cases, such as cruel dictators who mirror our desire to control others. It is equally applicable to groups of people as well as individuals. Criminals, for example, may represent the part of us that have a tendency to break agreements.

There are no exceptions with Radical Forgiveness. As I said in my first book, *Radical Forgiveness:* "If you can't forgive Hitler, you can't forgive anyone."

We use relationships as a way to create our experiences of separation. Then, through Radical Forgiveness, we heal the illusion of separation and become whole again. This process is as follows:

205

Stage 1: Two people are joined at the heart with the energy of Love flowing freely between them, knowing they are One and the same. There is no separation – only Oneness.

Stage 2: The agreement is made to separate vibrationally in order to experience the opposite of Oneness, allowing them to know Oneness as a feeling experience.

Separation is achieved by introducing judgments, expectations, demands, etc. These immediately block the Love that normally flows naturally between them. An endless attack and defense cycle is created based on victim consciousness, ensuring they stay separate for as long as needed before awakening.

Stage 3: Having experienced the amount of separation desired, they awaken. Through the process of Radical Forgiveness, they dissolve all the victim and perpetrator stories created by the judgments, demands and expectations. At that point, all blocks to the flow of Love are removed and the Love flows once more. In this drawing, I show Radical Forgiveness as a kind of transdermal patch we put on the skin to deliver medicine through the pores. We don't do anything directly to restore the flow of Love but simply apply the energy of Love over top of them. Hence the **"Radical Forgiveness Patch."**

207

We are likely to feel very differently about people after doing a Radical Forgiveness process around them. The people themselves, assuming you know them well enough, may become more likeable. This is because they no longer have to keep pushing your buttons for you. They can stop being a pain in the neck to you now, or they can move on.

Shown below is a worksheet to help you develop the habit of seeing the divinity in other people. If you use it often, starting with those you already have a dislike for, you will find yourself being much more tolerant of people in general. You will also exercise a lot more humility in the knowledge that it is always the case that the other person is you – God in all His many disguises.

Radical Acceptance

A Tipping Method Worksheet for Seeing the Divinity in Any Human Being

1. I recognize that I am finding it difficult to accept _____ as he/she is. The problem I have with him/her is:

_____

_____

2. The main feelings I am experiencing within myself right now as I bring this person to mind are: (Be totally honest and use <u>feeling</u> words.)

3. I honor my feelings and claim my right, as an awakened human being, to have these emotions and to be responsive to them. I value them because they give me good feedback about how I am seeing this person.

☐ AGREE   ☐ DISAGREE

4. Even though I am not aware of what it might be, I am open to the possibility that this person is in my life for a reason and perhaps is here to provide me a lesson or healing opportunity.

☐ AGREE   ☐ DISAGREE

5. I recognize that I may be using this person to not only create some fresh pain of separation within myself, but also to leverage one or more similar such instances of separation between myself and other important people in my life. For example:

_____

_____

I therefore recognize this person, from whom I have withheld love and who I have judged, as a soul-mate on a mission to awaken me to the truth of who I truly am, who he/she is, and who those are from whom I have withheld love previously. We are all part of the one Divine Essence.

☐ AGREE   ☐ DISAGREE

6. Even though I know there is no requirement that I like this individual as a human being, or approve his/her behavior in human terms, I am now willing to see the light in him/her and to know that the person's soul is Love, pure and simple, and he/she is, therefore, perfect in every way.

☐ AGREE   ☐ DISAGREE

7. I am feeling a sense of Oneness with this person now and feel gratitude for this person being in my life.

☐ AGREE   ☐ DISAGREE

Signed: _____ Date: _____

Application #17:

Survive Divorce and Move On to What's Next

Radical Forgiveness is the key to surviving divorce and moving on – leaving all the rancor and bad energy behind you. It's best for you, best for the children and best for your ex.

The more Radical Forgiveness you do during the divorce and after it, the better it will turn out for all concerned. Everything I said in the section on resolving disputes (Application #10) is applicable in the case of a divorce. After all, if it should happen to us, it will be the biggest exercise in dispute resolution any of us are likely to undertake.

The more you can bring an expanded consciousness to the situation, the better it will turn out, and the sooner you will be able to find a new partner to share your life with, assuming that this is still an attractive proposition for you.

I'm not going to say much about the process by which you use the Law of Attraction to manifest a new partner. That is mostly about Radical Manifestation, which, as a technique, is well covered in my book of the same name.

However, I do think you should look back at the sections in this book about evaluating an existing relationship (Application #13) and reconciling with a partner (Application #14). Apply all that information to how you would intend to build any relationship in the future, especially in terms of establishing agreements, values and boundaries. Let me spell this out for you by suggesting you follow these four rules before doing anything about creating a new relationship. [Note: These four rules are extracted from my book, *Expanding into Love*.]

Rule #1. Leave a significant amount of time between leaving one relationship and even thinking about creating another.

It takes a lot more time than you think to energetically disengage from the previous relationship, especially if it was deep and long-standing, and even more especially if the separation was painful. If there are children involved, the problem is compounded. If you leap straight into another relationship, the chances are very high that you will take into the new relationship all the unresolved issues you had in the old one, recreating the very same set of dynamics that might have been the cause of the breakup in the last relationship.

I realize, of course, that in many cases, meeting another person and falling in love with him or her may have precipitated the breakup. In that case, there might already be a new relationship in existence even before the old one is finished. Nevertheless, a wise couple will still arrange things so that each has a chance to live alone for a good while before moving in with each other. I would suggest at least 6 months and better yet one year for the reasons I give in Rule #4 below.

Men seem to have the greatest need to replace as quickly as possible, and often will force an earlier commitment than wisdom would normally dictate. He will be even more urgent if he is looking for a mother for his children, assuming he has any. So it will probably be the woman who has to resist the urge to move in together, and to insist on having the amount of time she needs to be alone. If he is not willing to allow that, then that should be a red flag. He's not worth having.

Even if it has been a number of years since your last relationship ended, and you have been wanting to manifest a new one for a while now, you may still need to do the forgiveness work on your previous partner. The fact that you may still have some energy left with your previous partner may be the very reason why you haven't been able to attract a new one.

Rule #2. *Do the forgiveness work on your previous partner before you begin manifesting a new one.*
And I don't mean just doing one Radical Forgiveness worksheet. Keep doing them or do the more intense, 21-Day Online Program for Forgiving Your Partner, until there is no energy left in the situation: no anger; no resentment; no jealousy; no pain; no regrets.

This takes work, obviously, but if you want your new relationship to work, it is essential that you release all those energies. This is why you need to have a lot of time on your own to do this work and to know who you are before you create the new one. There are many people who have never lived on their own for any length of time and, therefore, have no idea who they are separate from another. How can you expand into Love if you don't know who you are and feel less than whole without a partner?

Rule #3. *Be clear about what you want and don't want in a relationship.*

213

As I suggested in the opening paragraph of this chapter, refer back to Applications #13 and #14 to help you in this endeavor, or for a more in-depth treatment of this task, read the book *Expanding into Love*.

Then make a very exhaustive list of what you want and don't want. Put a lot of thought into listing all the attributes you want to have in the person. Think long and hard about what you feel are the most important things you will want in your relationship.

Rule #4. Scope your partner out over a period of at least 6 months before committing. Be a detective.
At first, the person you attract into your life may seem absolutely perfect. The problem is that once you have reached a certain stage of intimacy (into-me-see), and you have become hooked, the person begins to reveal the real man or woman behind the mask. Suddenly the person becomes quite opposite of what you thought and the relationship begins to look like a disaster. I can't tell you how many times I have heard the story of someone finding their 'soul-mate' – the perfect partner who is loving and caring – and then after six months they turn into a tyrant. There's a reason why this happens, but that's a whole other story. Just be warned that it is a very common scenario.

So, if you begin dating someone, stay alive to this possibility and do not commit to a full-fledged relationship until you have reached this stage in the relationship where you each have become comfortable enough with each other that you begin to be real. Watch out for any changes in his or her behavior.

They may be subtle at first, but there might be an outburst or two that will give you a hint of what may come later.

One of my clients who had experienced this 'personality switch' a couple of times felt determined not to have it happen again. She called the man's ex-wife and asked her what he was like deep down. His ex-wife was only too happy to tell her everything – both good and bad. She learned a lot from her, and they actually became quite good friends as a result. My client eventually married the guy, and it turned out fine. This is a risky strategy, but it is one way of finding out whether there is a hidden side to this person. You really don't know anyone until you live with them, so it's worth asking someone who has done so before you risk it yourself.

There are typically three possible ways in which people respond to this switch from 'soul-mate' to tyrant:

a) The first is to recognize that the new behavior crosses your boundaries and goes against your values, in which case you leave the relationship immediately.

b) The second is you commit to a further trial period to see if the behavior, now having been brought to the light, will disappear once you have done some further work with Radical Forgiveness in order to clear more of your own energy, have clearly stated your boundaries and made clear what you want and don't want.

The big trap here, though, is to imagine that you have the power to change the person. *You do not.* It is very common that women say to themselves, *"If I love him enough, he will*

215

change and become what I want him to be." It never happens, so please, abandon that strategy right away.

This option, then, is only viable if you are willing to watch to see if the behavior disappears completely within the 12-month period. If it does not, this means the relationship is potentially troubled, and you should consider letting it go.

c) The third option is to settle. This is when, because your need for a relationship is so strong, you are willing to put up with it so long as he/she stays with you. This option should only be taken if you wish to experience a lot more pain and suffering.

There's clearly a lot to learn in the process of surviving a divorce. The lessons to be learned were contained in the dynamics of the marriage itself. Make sure you give plenty of thought to what happened and why it was not possible to reconcile, even though you are now awake and have moved into the second phase of your life during which marriage takes on a different meaning.

Spend a lot of time alone. If possible, be single for a good while and don't even bother dating. Get to know who you are separate from being attached to someone else, and discover what is important to you in life and what your values are. If you have been co-dependent up to now, always putting the needs of others before your own, start putting your needs first.

If you have always been seeking approval from people, do the Radical Self Acceptance worksheet and find love and approval for yourself. If you've always felt you had to be perfect, practice letting that go. You are already perfect, just the way you are.

RESOURCES FOR THIS APPLICATION:
(Details in the Resources Section at the back of this book and at www.radicalforgiveness.com.)

Books:
Expanding into Love
Radical Manifestation

Worksheets:
Radical Manifestation Worksheet
Radical Forgiveness Worksheet
Radical Self-Acceptance Worksheet

Workshop: *Manifesting Your Perfect Mate*

Package: *QEMS Q-Work Kit*

Consultation: *By appointment*

25 Practical Uses for Radical Forgiveness:
Solving the Problems and Challenges of
Everyday Life in a New Way

PART FOUR

Applications for Practical Spirituality
at Work

18. Optimize Success in Business with
Radical Forgiveness

19. How to Rescue a Dysfunctional
Family Business

20. Shift Your Money Consciousness

Application #18:

Optimize Success in Business with Radical Forgiveness

Using Radical Forgiveness at work creates a more satisfying, joyful and rewarding work experience for everyone, making for a happier and more productive workforce.

Business owners, managers and executives should take note that one of the most potent uses of Radical Forgiveness is its deployment as a business management technique. It will improve overall performance, increase productivity, reduce attrition and boost profits, and will optimize the return on investment (ROI) in the people employed.

Business consultants who want to have a system to offer their clients that will alleviate employee problems like high attrition rates, frequent conflict and other issues that cost the company money, should pay attention too. There's a lot of potential here for enlightened consulting.

At the other end of the scale, individuals who find the environment in which they work stressful, negative, and vibrationally debilitating can use it to maintain a high vibration in spite of what is going on around them. Not only does it help them personally in this regard, but is likely to have the effect of slowly raising the vibration of those around him or her, without anything being said. It's an energy thing, you understand.

We refer to this as a 'stealth' method of slowly raising the vibration of one's own immediate working environment by the process of osmosis. The person with the highest vibration will always pull others in the same group up to that level eventually. In the person's immediate work environment, the result might be less complaining, fewer conflicts with colleagues, less finger pointing, more cooperation and so on. In a small company of 5 or 6 people, if the boss alone does it, the effect will be the same.

I know of a dentist who did Radical Forgiveness on his employees. Prior to this, his support staff were always complaining and being obstructive, and in one case embezzling money. They slowly became more cooperative and happy with each other. There were a couple who were of a lower vibration and did not change, but they left and were replaced by people of a higher vibration. His business went from strength to strength, and his office became a really nice place in which to work.

As time went on, each member of his staff became interested to know more and began using the tools, both for situations at work and at home. Now the whole team is very integrated and the energy flows easily and freely. The patients feel it too, so they have a much more pleasant experience than they expected to have at a dentist's office.

By the way, what we said in Application #10 about how an individual should use Radical Forgiveness to deal with bullies, authorities, neighbors and other individuals, as well as entities with whom you might be in dispute, applies in equal measure to co-workers, bosses, managers, and others you interact with in the workplace. It's no different in that sense.

But in this Application the emphasis is on how Radical Forgiveness affects the overall energy of the company, whether it is used just by the boss of a very small company, as in the above example of my dentist friend, or in a larger company where it is adopted as a management system. Here's how it works:

Every organization has a life force energy field of its own that is the sum total of the energy fields of every employee in the company, from the CEO down to the lowest paid worker. (It also includes customers, suppliers, consultants, regulators and so on, but let's keep the focus on the employees for now.)

It is in the interest of the company, therefore, to ensure that the energy field of every employee is as clear as possible and vibrating at a high rate. As we have seen, even if one employee carries a high energy rate, it will have the effect of pulling the overall energy of the organization up a notch or two.

The reverse is also true. Someone with a consistently low vibration will pull the overall vibration down. On the other hand, it may only be a temporary thing. An upset, a shock, a death in the family – anything can lower a person's vibration temporarily. Helping a person by taking them through a Radical Forgiveness process will help restore their energetic balance very quickly.

What if we could get a high proportion of the employees using the tools, as and when needed, in order to raise their personal vibration? Imagine the effect that would have on the overall vibration of the company energy field. Due to the Law of Resonance, the organization itself will follow suit. As a consequence, it will operate at a higher level than before. Everyone will benefit.

About a decade ago I wrote the book *Spiritual Intelligence at Work*. Since that time, I've developed a management technique and an employee development system based on the intentional use of the Radical Forgiveness technology in the work environment. It is called the Quantum Energy Management System (QEMS).

QEMS is best described as being a psycho-spiritual approach to increasing productivity, raising morale and preventing conflict in the workplace. But to be clear, it has nothing to do with religion. It is a secular activity that uses the part of our mind known as our Spiritual Intelligence.

[We have spoken of SI in previous chapters, but just to recap, Spiritual Intelligence is a faculty of mind we all possess in equal proportion. Even though it follows naturally from mental and emotional intelligence, it is not generally well understood or acknowledged. Nevertheless, when it is utilized it opens up a whole new way of being, interacting and living. As far as the world of work is concerned, it has enormous potential for good.]

As you might expect, the core technology of QEMS is a version of Radical Forgiveness appropriate for use in any work environment. It is encouraged through the use of a number of specially designed Q-WorkTools that we make available to employees online.

Everyone in the organization benefits enormously when this technology is used – even if used only by the top management at first. It optimizes productivity, raises morale, prevents conflict, reduces turnover, and increases profit. It also creates a more satisfying, joyful and rewarding work experience for everyone, making for a happier and more productive workforce.

However, it is a top-down system. If the CEO does not believe in it and use it, no one else will. It cannot be introduced as just another HR program. It has to come from the top. Leadership from that level is crucial.

The Problem It Solves
It was pointed out in earlier chapters that repressed feelings and unresolved issues cause energetic blocks that will lower a person's vibration considerably. Clearly, then, it is in the company's interest to give people the tools to clear such blocks to raise their vibration. A company that has a high vibration overall will, through the law of resonance, attract high vibration workers, high vibration suppliers and high vibration customers. Unfortunately, however, while machines and technical systems are by and large predictable, human beings are anything but. This is largely due to that negatively-charged, unconscious material we all carry with us to work, the stuff we have buried deep down in the subconscious mind. As I mentioned earlier, I have coined a special word for this - HUMENERGY.

Humenergy represents all the unconscious emotional baggage that everyone brings to work with them. In certain circumstances, this will be unconsciously acted out at work as

225

a way to release it. While this may be a good healing process for the person purging this humenergy as part of his or her awakening process, it can be disastrous for the organization.

For example, suppose someone in the corporation had a mother who was highly critical of him as a boy, while at the same time was also highly protective and quite smothering. As an adult, he managed to keep all his anger and frustration out of his awareness, safely tucked away in the dark recesses of his unconscious mind. This is what we all do with our childhood wounds.

But here's the risk in this strategy: We all have a built-in mechanism to heal such wounds, no matter how deep they reside in the unconscious mind, and no matter how unaware of them we are. Our Higher Self knows they are there – and that they need to be healed. So it looks around for an opportunity for our ego to act them out, unconsciously attracting someone into our life who has a similar energy to the person who wounded us. We then use that person as a way to resolve the underlying issue. The workplace is the perfect place to create such a healing drama.

Through the law of attraction, the employee will create some woman in authority over him who will be forceful and overwhelming, always checking on him to make sure he is doing his work. (Remember, there are no accidents, and we are creating our reality all the time.) This will echo his issue with his mother, giving him the opportunity to heal his wounds by getting back at his mother through that supervisor. (She may be the equivalent of the Friendly Soul in Neale Donald Walsch's story.)

Our man is likely to do everything he can to undermine her and make her life very difficult. He will subtly sabotage her work, and probably his too at the same time, assuming it will reflect badly on her if he performs badly. He will not realize it of course. He will find all sorts of ways to cover his tracks and make it look like it's all her fault. This can cost the company huge amounts of money, especially if the woman in question is a highly paid competent executive who leaves the company as a result of the sabotage. The cost of replacing and training a key executive is enormous. Attrition is one of biggest personnel problems that companies face today.

Don't imagine this will only happen to the odd individual. It's likely to happen to all of us in one way or another when the time is right. Healing dramas will typically show up in the corporate energy field as a sudden conflict, or as an unpleasant situation between people or groups of people. They can be sudden flare-ups or ongoing situations that never seem to get

227

resolved. It can involve sabotage, resistance to change, finger pointing, attrition, an increase in sick days taken, and so on.

Since this all happens way below the surface of everyday reality, those involved are unaware they are even creating these dramas, yet they cause severe interference in the energy flow of the corporation. This is quite incidental and of no (conscious) consequence to the players trying to heal each other. However, it matters a great deal to the corporation and it could certainly have grave consequences for the careers of the players in these healing dramas. This phenomenon needs to be recognized for what it really is. Not just a personality clash, disagreement over some policy or just another conflict, it's a perfectly normal healing drama. It is, in fact, Spiritual Intelligence in action.

Here is a fundamental truth about workplace conflict: *WE ARE NEVER UPSET FOR THE REASON WE THINK.* That's why it does not yield to traditional conflict resolution procedures. The conflict at hand is not the issue. It is always humenergy being acted out.

A person who has an issue with a male manager, for example, may well be subconsciously acting out his unresolved issue with his authoritarian father. An executive who gets promoted and then underperforms and perhaps even does damage may be acting out a core negative belief he has carried since childhood that he will never amount to much in life. The promotion will have triggered the sabotage response in order that he come back into alignment with that belief. The sabotage will be heavily disguised, and others will be blamed and scapegoated. It can take the form of making sure others in his/her department don't do well, or by hiring people who will be substandard.

Before Radical Forgiveness, repackaged as the Quantum Energy Management System (QEMS) came along, there was no way to deal with the problem of unconscious humenergy being acted out at work. Most companies don't even recognize the problem, or if they do, they just assume human beings are naturally volatile and unpredictable. They regard some negative behavior as an inevitable cost of doing business.

In reality, the cost has been enormous. You only have to take a look at the cost of treating one person in an Employee Assistance Program to know that. And the outcome seldom justifies the expense.

An unhappy or disgruntled executive can easily be lured away by a head hunting firm with offers of more money – though money is seldom the reason they leave. It costs a fortune to replace an executive, and it can take more than a year to bring a replacement up to speed. Add to these big-ticket costs the money wasted on all the day-to-day negative behavior occurring all the time as a result of people processing unconscious material by acting it out at work. Soon you can clearly add up the cost of humenergy.

Savvy business owners now realize that allowing such spontaneous healing dramas to develop creates major problems for the company. It makes sense to give a person who seems to have been triggered by something at work some simple tools that will help resolve the real issue underneath the apparent upset. This is what QEMS is for. Someone with a trained eye will see what is happening and will immediately suggest an appropriate tool, such as a worksheet or audio, before things get out of hand.

The wonderful thing about this method is that there is no need to find out what the underlying issue was that is being played out. Remember, the person who 'caused' the upset simply represents the person we were mad at as a child. Just doing a Radical Forgiveness worksheet will automatically create healing all the way back to the original event. This happens because the work collapses the overall energy field that has held that issue together all through the years, containing all the events like it all the way down the time line.

The tools are slightly modified to suit the typical corporate culture but they retain all the same principles of Radical Forgiveness. Instead of calling it a Radical Forgiveness Worksheet, we call it The Balancing Humenergy Worksheet. The Audio version is The 13 Step Process for Balancing Humenergy. We call them the Q-Work Tools.

The Q-Work Tools are designed to be used whenever the person becomes upset, dissatisfied about something, angry or judgmental. They are extremely simple and quick to use but, as we know, their effects are extraordinary. They enable the person to release the emotional energy invested in the situation before it gets too much of a hold, and in that way prevents a conflict from escalating, or even beginning. The situation causing the upset itself is invariably diffused as well. The Q-Work Tools work NOT at the psychological level but at the spiritual level, so the work happens below the level of conscious awareness. There is no psychotherapy involved.

In addition to increased profits and better relationships with customers, suppliers, vendors, strategic partners and other key stakeholders, the result is likely to be a reduction in internal conflict and dissent, an increase in morale and productivity, less absenteeism, improved turnover rates and increased productivity. It proves, and gives new meaning to, the old adage that a happy workforce is a productive workforce.

This use of the Radical Forgiveness technology is spelled out in much more detail in my book, *Spiritual Intelligence at Work*.

In addition to explaining the rationale for bringing the technology of Radical Forgiveness into management science, this book contains a fictitious story written to illustrate how humenergy can endanger a company. It is a cautionary tale that every executive, business manager and business owner should heed, for it can make the difference in the business's very survival. It is a dramatic illustration of how our unconscious humenergy can literally bring a company to its knees without anyone involved understanding how or why it happened.

The narrative tracks five key people in a small manufacturing company called GiCo, Inc.: the CEO, the PA to the CEO, the VP of Sales and Marketing, the Production Manager and the Production Supervisor. Each of their personal histories is explored, showing how these determine what they bring to the table in the way of unconscious humenergy. It illustrates how this affects the company, preventing it from growing and even threatening its very existence.

The Benefits

Implementation of QEMS results in: increased profits; better relationships with customers, suppliers, vendors, strategic partners and other key stakeholders; a reduction in internal conflict and dissent; an increase in morale and productivity; less absenteeism; improved turnover rates; and increased productivity. It gives new meaning to the idea that a happy workforce is a productive workforce.

If some employees do leave within 6 - 12 months of QEMS being introduced, they are usually those with a low vibration who were bringing the overall vibration of the company down. So it is nearly always for the best. They quickly become replaced by people with a higher vibration. Like attracts like. These new hires will be attracted by the high vibration of the company as a whole. They, in turn, will contribute to raising the vibration even higher. The beneficial effect is cumulative.

Top Down Only

The only caveat I always make concerning the likelihood of QEMS being used to successfully raise the overall vibration of the company is that it must be enthusiastically embraced, supported and used by the CEO and the top tier of management. It is not a system to be introduced at the HR level. Human Resource people should be involved in the dissemination of material and training, but embracing the system itself must come from the top.

RESOURCES FOR THIS APPLICATION:
(Details in the Resources Section at the back of this
book and at www.radicalforgiveness.com.)

Books:
Hidden Agendas at Work
Spiritual Intelligence at Work

Worksheet: *Balancing Humenergy* Worksheet

Package: *The QEMS Q-Work Kit*

Consultation: *By appointment*

Application #19:

How to Rescue a Dysfunctional Family Businesses

When you mix the emotional and tribal dynamics of an extended family with the economic demands and complexities of a business, without Radical Forgiveness both are likely to become casualties.

As we saw in the previous application, every business has its own overall energy field and is the sum total of the energy fields of each individual person in the business... plus customers, venders, inspectors and so on. It continually changes over time according to changing circumstances.

Families also have energy fields. They might be composed of parents, grandparents, children, in-laws, aunts, uncles, and so on. Depending on the ages and stages of development of each individual member of the family, its energy field will be very dynamic and constantly changing. It's not easy to maintain a good energetic balance in a family. The bigger it gets the more it has to change and adapt.

In a family-run business, it is highly likely that these 'business' and 'family' fields become all mixed together. That can spell trouble, especially if the family is in any way dysfunctional. (Show me one that isn't!)

Families and businesses are different energies that don't always mix easily. The wider and deeper they become, the worse it is. Husband and wife teams can work quite well, assuming the marriage itself is strong, but if it goes wide by including siblings, in-laws, and other relatives, you increase the likelihood of power struggles. This also applies if it goes deep by adding a generation or two.

The trick with a family-run business, then, is to keep the two fields as separate as possible... or at least to be aware of the difference between them.

My job when I go into a family-run business is to first draw a diagram of the energy field of the business. I map the energy flowing between people, whether it is negative or positive, and show which people have the most power in directing the energy at this time. I also want to see how those dynamics change when circumstances change, or how they are likely to change in the near as well as distant future.

That gives me a picture of the energetic structure of the company and how the energy is flowing throughout. I am interested to see how the four main forms of energy are flowing – money, information, materials and human energy.

It is the last of these which is the most problematic. People are emotional beings and are unpredictable. As members of the same family, they also carry a lot of emotional baggage. They hide their motives, their wounds and their grievances, but they act them out from time to time, usually to the detriment of the business.

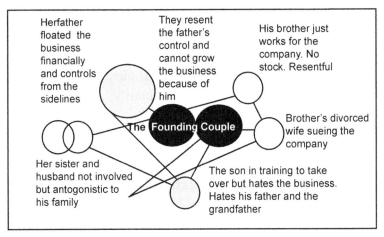

Fig. 12. *The Family Energy Map*

After mapping the business energy field, I construct a diagram of the family energy field. It includes not only those running or working in the business, but those with financial or other interests. Again, I follow the energy and plot the dynamics that seem to be operating within the whole field. It often takes a lot of careful digging to find out what is really going on within the family. I have to build a lot of trust with everyone.

237

Once I have both fields mapped out, it becomes a matter of laying one over the other to see how they interact with each other. Where do the energies get mixed? Who stirs the pot and why? Where are power struggles likely to occur? And so on.

This process results in a complex 3-dimensional model, which I then attempt to disentangle. The goal is to get to a point where the two energy fields are as separate as they possibly can be. It is often a long job, depending on the size of the company and how many family members are involved.

At that point, I decide where I need to direct my energies and what problems need to be solved. These are invariably rooted in the basic family dynamics, but problems can also become evident in how the business is structured. And, as with any business energy field, there may be problems with people who are employees unconnected to the family.

Needless to say, Radical Forgiveness is the answer to most of the family problems which are creating all the other problems. Getting everyone on board with this methodology is the biggest challenge. It has to come from the top.

The owner or CEO has to want it and be willing to work it. It usually involves some training, but once people understand the Quantum Energy Management System, they have no difficulty working with it. Once they see the results in their own lives and the difference it makes to the business in terms of efficiency, productivity, workplace harmony and profitability, they go for it.

However, this is one area in which Radical Forgiveness cannot be done as a self-help exercise. Everyone is too closely involved and cannot see the forest for the trees. If the business is going south because of the dysfunction, everyone is scared and in survival mode. For these reasons, it is nearly always necessary to have a consultant work with the company to turn things around.

RESOURCES FOR THIS APPLICATION:
(Details in the Resources Section at the back of this book and at
www.radicalforgiveness.com.)

Worksheet: *Radical Forgiveness* Worksheet

Online Programs:
"Breaking Free." A 21-Day Program for Forgiving Your Parents
"Family Matters." A 21-Day Program for Forgiving Your Siblings
"Great Expectations." A 21-Day Program for Forgiving Your Kids.
"Moving Forward," A 21-Day Program for Forgiving Your Partner.

Package: *Q-Work QEMS Kit*

Application #20:

Shift Your Money Consciousness

Money is our greatest teacher. If we can master the true meaning of money, we can master anything. And that has nothing to do with how much of it we have or don't have. It's about how we feel about it that is the key.

A t first blush you might wonder why I am putting money and Radical Forgiveness together. Consider how often we feel victimized in relation to money and you'll realize how connected these two things are. An awful lot of misery over money issues can be overcome if we apply both Radical Forgiveness and Radical Self-Forgiveness to the problems raised by it. A lot of marriages can be saved and business bust-ups prevented by applying these two technologies to most issues relating to money.

Since it is necessary for everyone to have it as the means of exchange for the things they need or desire, no one can escape from it or the problems it creates. Everyone is touched by money, whether they have a lot or very little... and regardless, everyone wants more.

Few people are ever satisfied with the amount of money they have. But the more we have, the more fearful we are of losing it. We measure ourselves by how much we have or don't have. We measure the worth of others by how much they have, and we make judgments about them based on what they do with it.

Nothing comes close to money in matching its propensity to create fear, envy, guilt, resentment, jealousy, rage, hate, hostility, etc., in virtually everyone on the planet. Enemies are constantly being created because of it. People will commit terrible crimes for money. People are betrayed over it, cheated out of it, even killed over it. We are victimized because of it all the time. People create countless ways to have us part with our money. Capitalism as an economic system actually depends on making us victims over money. It wouldn't work otherwise.

Clearly then, there are plenty of opportunities for us to practice Radical Forgiveness on those who victimize us over money, and just as many for us to practice Radical SELF-forgiveness. After all, how many times have we felt the need to forgive ourselves for being vulnerable enough or even stupid enough to get cheated, conned, exploited or overcharged? How many times have we risked our money and lost it? How often have we failed to manage our money properly and found ourselves in serious trouble over it? How many times have we cheated someone else out of money, or been dishonest in some way in order to avoid parting with money, and felt bad about it? Many, many times, I'm sure.

But now that you know how to use both technologies, you have the means to reduce the pain and suffering around being hurt by someone over money. It's no different from any other form of victimization. As in Radical Grieving, for example, the pain and suffering depends on how you think (radically) about death. The extent to which you suffer from money problems depends on how willing you are to think radically about money.

Just as the philosophy of Radical Forgiveness is based on a very different paradigm of reality than conventional forgiveness, the same is true of money. The old paradigm about money is that it is in very short supply and there isn't enough to go around. We have to work hard to get it, and only certain types of people are entitled to have a lot of it. We all have our own set of limiting beliefs about money that conform to this old paradigm, and it is those that cause us all the suffering around money.

The new paradigm says there is no shortage of money. There is plenty of it in the world. If you are open to receive it, you can attract it to you quite easily.

Money is simply energy, so it is subject to the same set of laws that govern all energy in the Universe. It will move in any direction the laws of attraction or repulsion direct it to move.

It will always show up when we need it so long as we don't block it. It is entirely neutral and does not judge or discriminate who should have it or why. It has no power in itself and no meaning other than what we decide to give it. It has no value other than what we decide to exchange it for.

Our resistance is so great to thinking of money in this way and letting go of our fear of it, it undermines our willingness to accept and live by the paradigm suggested by Radical Forgiveness. The central tenet of the new paradigm is that the Universe is always taking care of us and giving us what we need when we need it.

If we don't trust that idea when it comes to money, then we really don't trust the Universe. This is why money is our greatest teacher. If we can master money in this way, we can master anything. And that has nothing to do with how much of it we have or don't have. It's how we feel about it that is the key.

In my book, *Radical Manifestation, The Fine Art of Creating the Life You Want,* I listed some of the characteristics I would expect to see in people who have mastered money. They are as follows:

• A complete disregard for money as an end in itself.

They realize that money has no inherent value beyond the meaning people give it. The meanings people attach to money are all related to the old paradigm to which they don't subscribe. For example: money means security; money equals power; money connotes success; and so on. These people are not willing to give money the power to define them, nor to run their lives.

• A love of the freedom money gives them to make choices.

This is the only meaning they are willing to give money. For as long as they have some, it does give them freedom to make choices, even if the range is limited. With more money, more choices are available. However, they realize that it is the choices one makes that determine happiness, not the amount of money.

• A seemingly natural ability to attract money.

You've met people like this, I know. They are money magnets. Money just flows to them. However, not all of them are people you would automatically associate with the new paradigm. The kind of people I am thinking about would be the ones who easily attract money, but who also satisfy the other criteria.

• **A heightened state of openness to receive money.**

This is different from the previous paragraph in that this refers to a kind of allowing that comes from knowing that money has no meaning, that it is neutral and has no power in and of itself. Money is devoid of any issues of deservability, responsibility, worthiness to receive, or fear. These are people who simply have a state of pure openness to receive.

• **A high need to share it abundantly with others.**

They feel no need to hold onto money and get a real kick out of giving it away in good measure. This is different from the kind of tithing where people give in the expectation of getting more back than they gave, or where they give to get a tax break. It is giving out of the sheer joy of giving, knowing that there's plenty more in the spiritual pipeline.

• **A desire to make it work for the common good.**

They understand the idea of money as energy and the difference it can make when directed in ways that serve humanity, the planet, the animal kingdom and all of life.

- **A firm belief in the abundance of the Universe.**

This is the core idea, and it is non-negotiable. Without this one idea as the anchor, none of the others would have meaning. It is the core belief within the new paradigm. Without this, it is nothing.

- **An unshakable trust that their needs will always be met.**

This arises out of the solid belief that abundance is the natural condition of the Universe. It indicates a willingness to put that to the test at any time.

- **A complete absence of any attachment to having money, knowing that it will manifest when needed – and it always does.**

The person who operates in this way is truly free – free from the need to have more money than he/she needs – and is totally at peace in the knowledge that whether money arrives or not, all is well.

As you would imagine, these people are quite rare. If you look at that list again, you will see that each one of the characteristics depends upon the person's consciousness being grounded in the new paradigm. Of these nine characteristics, the first six could be applied to people operating in either paradigm or straddling both at the same time. The last three, however, have no such flexibility in their definition. They are as fundamental to the new paradigm as they are poison to the old one.

Just as shifting our thinking about death and dying reduces our suffering and makes grieving less about the dying and more about the missing, so shifting our thinking about money will make both the process of forgiveness and self-forgiveness a whole lot easier. It will simply be about the betrayal, the con or whatever occurred to make you mad. It won't be about the money, though.

Since money is not in short supply, and you can attract it to you whenever you need it, you cannot lose it. No one can really take away from you anything that is in abundant supply and readily available. There may be some inconvenience caused if you are without it for a while, and that may be irritating, but you will not be obsessing about losing money. You won't have lost it. You will have abandoned all the meanings you once gave it, and it will no longer define you. It has no power over you.

That said, working this new money paradigm is every bit as challenging as working with the Radical Forgiveness paradigm. What I always say about Radical Forgiveness applies to the new money consciousness. *Fake-it-'til-you-make-it*. Don't worry about having to believe it.

The flip side, however, is that you must use the tools we provide for you to make it work. They are essential. Otherwise your head will intervene to block you, just like it has in the past. All those old limiting beliefs that live in your subconscious mind will come flooding back to sabotage you.

Suppose, for example, someone has cheated you out of some money. You will do a Radical Forgiveness worksheet on that person, but at the same time you would need to do a Money Consciousness worksheet. This will shift the energy both ways.

247

Practice doing it with some issues that are not too challenging at first, just so you can feel the difference and experience the level of success that might come. You may be very surprised at the results.

Do the same thing if you blame yourself for getting in a financial bind, by combining a Radical Self-Forgiveness worksheet and a Money Consciousness worksheet.

When you do a Radical Manifestation worksheet and money is part of what you want to create, use the Money Consciousness worksheet in tandem with it. It's a process, but it works. If you think you have some strong resistance to having money flow easily in your life, you might also wish to do the Online Money Program.

Finally, let me add that if we do have a world-wide financial crisis and all the systems for keeping money flowing collapse, then obviously the level of inconvenience will increase. But if you can maintain a high level of trust that you will be provided for, even without money working as the means of exchange, you will get through it. If this does happen (and it is not an unlikely scenario), that's when we will learn how little meaning money has in reality. We will then learn that the only real currency is Love for one another and a willingness to share.

RESOURCES FOR THIS APPLICATION:
(Details in the Resources Section at the back of this
book and at www.radicalforgiveness.com.)

Book: *Radical Manifestation*

Worksheets:
Radical Forgiveness Worksheet
Radical Self-Forgiveness/Self-Acceptance Worksheet
Money Consciousness Worksheet
Radical Manifestation Worksheet

Online Programs:
Radical Manifestation Program
X4 Radical Money Program

25 Practical Uses for Radical Forgiveness:
Solving the Problems and Challenges of
Everyday Life in a New Way

PART FIVE

Death, Tragedy and Other Illusions

21. Making Your Radical Forgiveness
    Bucket List

22. Grieving the Loss of A Loved One
    with Less Pain

23. Making Sense of Abortion

Application #21:

Making Your Radical Forgiveness Bucket List

If you forgive everyone you need to forgive, and clear up any remaining issues with family and friends before you die, it will give you a better chance of dying peacefully and without pain.

In Part One I clearly stated that toxic mental, emotional and even negative spiritual energy is bad for your health. It is also very bad for your death.

If you die while still holding resentment or other forms of non-forgiveness, you will take it with you. You will not be free of it. You will have to deal with it on the other side, and there's no guarantee it will be any easier. Your energetic connection with the one you haven't forgiven yet will not be as direct as when you were both on the earth plane, making it much harder to break free.

Not only will you be burdened by the crappy energy you take with you, so will the person you haven't forgiven, assuming it mattered to them. Any amends they might have made while you were alive are now impossible. It becomes unfinished business and that makes it even more toxic that it was before. Start the Radical Forgiveness process now with those who are alive to allow you both a more peaceful transition.

Though it is more difficult, Radical Forgiveness can be done with those who have transitioned. At one point in our

253

Radical Forgiveness healing intensive known as the *Miracles Workshop*, participants do one hour of 'Satori' breathwork. They all lie on the floor with their eyes closed, music playing, and engage in conscious circular breathing. In effect, it is intentional hyper-ventilating. A lot of healing takes place while they are in the altered state induced by the breathwork. It is not unusual for participants who focus their forgiving on someone who has already transitioned to make contact with that person's spirit-being.

Those that do this work nearly always report that the spirit-being of the person who has already transitioned expresses deep gratitude for the energy of forgiveness directed towards them. It enables the spirit-being to release their pain as well. These spirit-beings indicate that the unhealed energy that existed at the time of their death became a cord that bound them to the earth plane longer than necessary, making it more difficult for them to move further into the light.

This was compounded many times over if the lack of forgiveness or even hatred was mutual. What happens in the breathwork session, then, is that the cord is cut and that energy is dispersed. The person doing the Radical Forgiveness here on the earth plane feels a sense of freedom and joy, while the spirit is released from the bondage and attachment to this vibration and is free to move on.

Clearly, both parties suffer when one dies and the other is left behind with unhealed energy of resentment, anger, jealousy, sadness, guilt, etc. Both are held captive.

This being the case, it is obvious that you stand to gain much by doing all the forgiveness work you can with those who are still alive, as well as on those who are now dead. You need to do it while you still have breath in your body and the mental capacity to remember who it is you need to forgive and why.

If you have someone in mind who died without healing an outstanding feud, disagreement, wound or whatever else might have disrupted the love between you, you owe it to yourself and to that departed person to do the Radical Forgiveness process around that issue immediately.

I doubt whether there is a person on the planet that does not have some reason to forgive their parents, and this is no less true if the parents are already dead. The parent/child relationship is characterized by conflict. Remember, we chose our parents to give us our first and most intense experience of separation. If they are dead, do a worksheet on them. If they are still alive, do a worksheet on them. Clear as much remaining energy as you can.

If you are a parent yourself, you may need to forgive your kids for some things as well, like their rebellion as teenagers, resistance to your rules, drug use, moving away and depriving you of access to your grandchildren and so on. We don't often talk about forgiving our own children, but in my experience the pain they can cause can be every bit as hurtful as the abuse children suffer from parents. I have itemized this as one of the 25 practical uses for Radical Forgiveness. (See Application #12.)

Another reason to forgive everyone and clear up any remaining issues with family and friends before you die is that it will give you a better chance of dying peacefully and without pain.

I first observed this phenomenon when working with cancer patients in the 90's.

As I pointed out in Application #4, cancer patients are notorious for holding onto resentment and grief and seldom ever forgive on their own. The tension this pent-up energy creates in the body is enormous. It stands to reason that if the body is tight and full of long-held emotional energy, death is likely to be painful and less than peaceful, because holding on tight is, for cancer patients, the norm. I am quite sure that this holds true for anyone who dies while still refusing to release their negative emotions and beliefs. If you hold onto that stuff, your body will hold on too, and death will not come easy.

If you've got any sense at all, you don't wait until the day before you die to make a will. Even if you are healthy and well, we all know that death can come at any moment. Making a forgiveness list and working your way through it is no different than making a will or creating a bucket list of all you want to do before you die.

It's worth doing anyway, of course, for all the other reasons given in this book, but it will likely make a big difference in how you die, and whether or not you get stuck in the void between the worlds waiting for someone down here to cut the cords. You might wait many generations. So for your own sake and for those who are important to you, do the forgiveness work now, before the grim reaper comes knocking. Like I said, it's no different to making a bucket list and a will. You are simply ensuring a safe passage to the other side for yourself and others.

RESOURCES FOR THIS APPLICATION:
(Details in the Resources Section at the back of this
book and at www.radicalforgiveness.com.)

Worksheet: *Radical Forgiveness* Worksheet

Workshop: *'Miracles' Weekend Workshop*

Package: *Radical Forgiveness Ceremony-in-a-Box*

Application #22:

Grieving the Loss of a Loved One with Less Pain

We don't allow ourselves time to grieve to the extent we should, given the intensity of the suffering a death can cause and how toxic that energy can become if it is not felt and fully expressed.

One of the things we love to do and have done in many places all around the world is the Radical Forgiveness Ceremony. It's a wonderful way to have large groups of people forgive themselves and everyone else in their lives all in the space of a couple of hours.

What we do in the ceremony is ask a series of questions that cover the full range of how people might have been victimized. People respond to the ones that apply to them personally by walking across a circle in order to release the pain associated with the issue raised. They find a partner on the way, connect physically and say to each other, "I'm sorry that happened to you." After a quick hug, they then complete the journey across the circle.

Invariably, there are a couple of questions that are virtually guaranteed to evoke tears in many of the participants. The question that pertains to the subject of this chapter is one of them. It is: *"If you have ever lost anyone, a person or a pet even, to an unexpected, untimely or tragic death, including suicide, walk the circle."* It's not surprising that so many walk the circle on this one, since there are few people who have not felt the pain of losing someone close to them at some time in their lives.

When death of a loved one, or even a pet, comes gently and quite naturally at the end of life, we can prepare ourselves for it and deal with the loss without too much anguish. But if the death is premature, tragic, accidental, unexpected or self-inflicted, the grief can be excruciating. Children who lose their parents at a young age may carry that loss all through their lives.

Many children experience the loss of a pet before they lose a parent, so grief can come early for many of them. Death is a constant presence in our lives and few escape what Stephen Levine called, 'the rope-burn of grief.'[1]

While the loss of a loved one is the most painful, we can suffer grief over the loss of anything that we held to be important in our lives. Losing a pet, a home, a job or one's own business can be devastating. The more we interpret it as losing part of our own identity and a measure of our self-worth, the worse we feel.

My grandfather, who was born into poverty in the East End of London, clawed his way up the ladder and eventually had his own flourishing business making hats in their basic form. They were then sent to Italy for finishing. As soon as war broke out with Germany and Italy, that link was severed. He was bankrupt virtually overnight. He had come from poverty and was plunged back into it again through no fault of his own. He was devastated and basically never got over it. He died in his early 60's of a heart attack, a bitter and grief-stricken man.

We don't do grief well in the western world. Compared to people in other parts of the world, we have very few rituals or customs that help us grieve. We don't allow ourselves time to grieve to the extent we should, given the intensity of the suffering a death can cause and how toxic that energy can become if it is not felt and fully expressed.

Grief is a process and we must give ourselves time to go through it. A soldier who loses a limb in the war will need to grieve the loss of the leg or arm before he or she can go on and adjust to life without it. A person who loses the job he has been in for years and given his life to will need to grieve it as well. Without grieving the old one, he won't be able to attract a new job that will suit him. Someone who loses a relationship must grieve the loss of that relationship before he or she can successfully create a new one. Otherwise, he or she will take the old energy into the new one and lose that one too.

When we started designing our Radical Grieving Online Program, we faced a dilemma. With all the other online programs, most of which are completed over 21 days, we make sure people have ample time to touch into all the emotions they have about their parents, their partners, their siblings and so on, before moving into the actual forgiveness process. But grief is different. You cannot make yourself move through grief in less time than it takes. For some it might take a few days, while for others it can take months, if not years. So it couldn't be a 21 Day program like many of the others.

Any program designed to help with grief must encourage and give space for feeling and expressing the pain of loss. That

261

is a given. Radical Grieving is not a way to short-circuit our grief. It is a way to transform it, and we do that by reducing the suffering. Let me explain how.

In an earlier application, I made the distinction between pain and suffering. Pain is the raw emotion and it is felt in the heart. Suffering comes on top of the pain of loss in the form of thoughts, ideas, beliefs, attitudes, prejudices, need to blame and so on.

And that's where Radical Forgiveness comes in. We can reduce our suffering simply by seeing the death from a Radical Forgiveness perspective. Instead of seeing it, as most people now do, as a failure, untimely, preventable, etc., we can ease the pain if we become open to the possibility that the death occurred when and how it was meant to happen. Also, by realizing that we have no right to judge it since it was of our soul's choosing, not ours. Even death by murder, if it were to happen, would be 'perfect' because we would have to assume our soul wanted that experience.

The other important assumption that has to be released is that death is real. It is not real. The soul is immortal. Only the body dies. It is simply a significant change in the frequency at which we vibrate that moves us from one state of being to another.

Once we have stopped defining grief as being remorse over the death itself, our suffering is greatly reduced. Our grief is then all about our unbearable loss, the pain of knowing that we will not have the person or pet in our lives anymore. Yes, that will take time to accept, but it is made a whole lot easier by letting go of all that other junk.

Even if this is not 100% true, deep down we know that there is at least a measure of truth in it. Why else would we say things like, *"When your number's up, that's it?"* That's no different to saying that destiny plays a big hand in when and how you die.

Most of us also know people who swear they had some circumstance in which they certainly would have died were it not for some unseen hidden hand that saved them. Perhaps you have had this experience yourself. Then there are many thousands of people who have had near-death experiences, who all come back with roughly the same story about feeling a loving presence that tells them it is not their time yet.

Much as it tries to, science cannot prove anything to the contrary. Some of the theories that scientists come up with are infinitely more outrageous, stupid and improbable than the ones they try to refute. This is not surprising since science is, by definition, the study of the physical universe. It is not equipped to even begin looking at what is essentially mystical and non-physical. It simply doesn't have the tools.

What to Do Next

If you have a copy of my book, *Expanding into Love,* read the chapter on "Grieving Your Losses." It goes into the idea of Radical Grieving in more depth than I do here. This exercise is included in that chapter:

a) Make a list of all the incidents in your life where death separated you from someone who was important to you. Then do the following.

i. On a scale of 1 - 10, estimate how much grief you felt (or feel) over losing this person (or pet.) 1 = hardly any at all, and 10 = intense grief and suffering.
ii. Who do you blame or hold responsible for the death?
iii. What feelings did you have immediately following the death?
iv. What judgments did you have about the death?
v. What feelings do you have now?

How you score this will vary according to the circumstances of the death. For example, if your mother died peacefully at age 95 after a long and happy life and was starting to get ill, your grief will be of a different order than if she died relatively young, having been killed by a hit-and-run driver. Parents who lose a child suffer a lot, because for a child to predecease its own parents seems out of the natural order of things.

b) If you blame someone or some institution for the death, or for not preventing it, you must do a Radical Forgiveness Worksheet on each of the people and/or institutions you blame, making sure you spend time on writing the reframe along the lines suggested in this application. (Use the statements in the exercise at the end of this application as a resource for good phrases to include in your reframe.)

c) Another option is the 3-Letter process. This process was outlined in Application #6 and is easily adapted to any situation.

d) If you feel some measure of responsibility for the person's passing, even if it is irrational, you must do a Radical Self-Forgiveness worksheet on yourself to clear that guilt.

e) It is not uncommon to feel anger towards the one who died, even if it was no fault of their own. Death feels to us very much like abandonment. Ironically, now that you know it was their choice to leave, you might feel even more justified in feeling angry about him or her leaving you to deal with the rest of your life alone. So, a Radical Forgiveness worksheet or the Three Letters on the dearly departed is probably going to be necessary. It is especially necessary if it was a suicide.

I should also stress that doing a worksheet on someone is not being disloyal or unfriendly. Energetically, you are doing it for them as much as for you, and in that sense it is a very loving thing to do. This is even more so if the person you are doing a worksheet on is dead. It releases them to move on.

f) Finally, do the Radical Grieving Online Program. Once you have purchased it, it is yours forever, so you can use it as many times as you wish.

Here is an exercise you can do immediately. It, too, is contained in the chapter "Grieving Your Losses" in *Expanding into Love.* The statements are drawn from the audio process, '13 Steps to Radical Grieving.'

Choose an event over which you are still grieving. After you have run through in your mind the circumstances of the death, remind yourself of his or her relationship with you and what he or she meant to you. Then read out loud, slowly and with awareness, each of the following statements:

1. In the wake of his/her death, I am allowing myself to feel how deeply I burn with grief over the loss. What a hole the loss has left in me! How my heart aches over the loss. I am focusing all my attention on the grief and allowing it to flow through my body. I am allowing the tears to come forth without restriction.

2. I claim my right to have such feelings and am willing to drop all judgments about my emotional state, knowing that no matter what I believe about death, it is essential that I feel my grief.

3. I am willing to see that a person's dying is an integral part of their life's journey, and the timing and circumstances of their death are all part of their divine plan and, at times, even a matter of choice. I am now willing to see that death is simply an illusion.

4. Knowing this now, I am willing to let go of all my judgments about this death and the circumstances in which it happened.

5. I am open to the idea that we all existed in spirit before we chose to take on a body as a way to purposely experience separation, and that I will continue to exist, albeit in a state of oneness, after my body has ceased to be.

6. I am willing to be open to the idea that the death I am grieving was in a sense perfect and was meant to happen in that way.

7. I am open to the idea that in my willingness to accept the person's death as perfect, in the spiritual sense, I am making the person's transition easier, more peaceful and harmonious than it would otherwise be were I to continue seeing it as tragic or wrong.

8. Even though I know I am going to miss him/her, I am nevertheless beginning to feel more peaceful and accepting of the death itself, knowing that it was his/her choice to become free of the burden of having a physical body and to go home.

9. I am now finding myself letting go of the need to see the death as anything less than perfect and beginning now to feel a sense of peace both for myself and for him/her.

10. Death is neither a failure nor an unnatural occurrence. Coming to an acceptance of death as part of life itself brings a deeper meaning to our sense of loss and ultimately is the balm that heals our grief. As I now release him/her from any further need to be energetically attached to me, I am beginning to feel a little more peaceful now.

And so it is.

RESOURCES FOR THIS APPLICATION:
(Details in the Resources Section at the back of this book and at www.radicalforgiveness.com.)

Book: *Expanding into Love*

Online Program: *Radical Grieving (includes the 13 Steps to Radical Grieving Audio)*

Package: *The Radical Forgiveness Ceremony-in-a-Box*

Application #23:

Making Sense of Abortion

*Disappointment notwithstanding, I cannot imagine that
the soul is mortally wounded if the mother
says 'No,' even if it has already anchored
itself in the form we call a fetus.
Even if it was aborted, it
would not be extinguished.
The soul cannot die.*

In the previous pages I made mention of the Radical Forgiveness Ceremony, in which we invite people to walk the circle in response to any question about which they have residual pain. One of those questions is about abortion. It goes like this. *"If you ever had to agonize over, or be party to the decision, whether or not to have an abortion, walk the circle."*

Typically we see about 30-40% of all those participating in the ceremony walking the circle for this one, including a lot of men. This gives you some idea why it deserves its own application in this book, and shows how much forgiveness needs to done around this issue.

The words in the question are carefully chosen. Take the word agonize. Deciding whether or not to have an abortion is agonizing for most people faced with the question. It is made all the more agonizing because of the external polarized religious and political pressures that are brought to bear on the issue. This can magnify the stress to a very high degree.

269

Notice, too, the words 'party to.' It is important that we do not ignore how difficult the decision is for the man as well as the woman, though in the end it is she who has to decide. It's her body.

That said, I think, in general, men should honor that fact and stop pontificating about something they cannot and will never understand. They have no way of knowing what it is like to have the spiritual responsibility for giving life to a soul that requests to come through. Only a woman knows. Men should have enough humility to admit that they are not privy to the same knowledge as women, and should be willing to defer to feminine wisdom when it comes to the process of giving life.

Nevertheless, the ideal for a couple is that the decision is a joint one. It should be borne in mind, however, that it is likely the man will use very different criteria in his mind to those used by the woman. His approach is likely to be pragmatic and analytical, weighing the pros and cons mainly from an economic point of view, as well as how it will affect him and his relationship with his partner. Her approach will have some of that, but it will primarily be governed by how she feels. For her, it is an emotional decision.

If the woman is under-age, and/or not married or in a committed relationship, then the parents may be involved in the decision. The potential for drama in that case is very high.

Depending on the circumstances, a lot of forgiveness will be called for on everybody's part, but here I am focusing on the one who is thinking of having, or has had, an abortion. For example:

1. Forgiving yourself for getting pregnant in the first place;

2. Forgiving the man for getting you pregnant in the first place;

3. Forgiving the man for not supporting you in your decision;

4. Forgiving the man if he puts undue pressure on you to abort;

5. Forgiving those who brought pressure on you one way or the other on religious or political grounds;

6. Forgiving the makers of the contraceptives that failed you;

7. Forgiving the male-dominated church for shaming you and others in your situation;

8. Forgiving the politicians for making it a political issue and exploiting your situation;

9. Forgiving family members and parents for shaming you and not supporting your decision.

Abortion is likely to bring up a wide range of emotions: guilt, shame, fear, anger, sadness, resentment, frustration, disappointment and grief. I mention grief particularly because abortion is often experienced by the woman as a profound loss, especially if she is unable to conceive again and feels she has missed out on the chance to have children biologically. This can be a feeling that lasts a lifetime. If this is true for you or someone you know who is suffering in this way, the Online Radical Grieving Program will be very helpful.

Guilt and shame are the other two big ones. The flames of these negative emotions are vigorously fanned by the religous zealots and the political opportunists. Radical Self-Forgiveness will be called for in this case and, if the free worksheets are not sufficient to break through the guilt and shame, the Online Self-Forgiveness/Self-Acceptance Program will be the one to use.

Unfortunately, the issue of abortion has become extremely polarized. On one side, there are those who oppose it under any circumstances; and on the other side are those who feel it is a personal choice. There seems not to be much in between, though I think most people would have a more nuanced position if left to make their own decision about it.

This is not say, however, that abortion should be treated lightly, no matter what our thoughts are about the morality of it and the ethical issues it raises. It is certainly worthy of our deep consideration on ethical, social and spiritual grounds.

But the fact is, no one has the right to impose on other people the position they wish to take on abortion because neither they nor anyone else, not even the church, has the answer to the only question that matters. That is, when and how does the soul enter the body, and what happens to it if the pregnancy is terminated?

This is an extremely important question for us to examine in this part of the book, because it will color our whole approach to doing the forgiveness work required to bring about the relief we might be looking for if abortion is our issue.

We cannot look to science for the answer, for while it tells us all about the intricacies of fertilization and cell division, it has nothing to say about the process of incarnation.

Religion is no help either since it just metes out dogma and takes up a fixed position based on prejudice but is no better informed about the intricate process whereby a soul attaches to a physical body than anyone else. Politicians are even worse. They just see abortion as a wedge issue on which to unashamedly campaign for votes. They simply exploit the uncertainty and use fear and shame to keep the issue polarized along party lines. Shame on them, I say.

We can only guess how we transition between the spiritual and physical realms through the processes of birth and death. However, as I have written elsewhere, I feel there is enough evidence out there to at least suggest, if not actually prove beyond a shadow of a doubt, that we reincarnate over and over again, and that death is just a process whereby we transition between the physical and spiritual realms by altering our vibration. Therefore, the soul is immortal and cannot be killed, either while in the womb or at any time afterwards.

Though this is not license to commit murder, it does seem to me that while the fetus is in the very early stages of development in the womb of a woman, it is her choice as to whether to accept the responsibility of giving it life in a human body or saying to the soul, *"No, not now. I am not ready for it. There are good reasons why it would not be good.*

273

Go back home to the spiritual realm and either try coming back later or find another woman who wants a child and will fit your needs."

Now, I can easily imagine the soul might be very disappointed if the woman refuses. After all, that soul may have given a lot of thought to why that person was the ideal parent through which to experience life. It may even have had an agreed soul contract between it and the soul of the mother.

But disappointment notwithstanding, I cannot imagine that the soul is mortally wounded if the mother says 'No,' even if it has already anchored itself in the form we call a fetus. If it were to be aborted, it would not be extinguished. The soul cannot die. It simply goes back home to the spiritual realm, in all probability, no worse for wear but perhaps having experienced something instructive and valuable.

And who is to say that the soul did not choose to have the abortion experience in order to balance the energy of having been a woman who aborted a fetus in a previous life or to allow the woman's soul the experience of deciding whether or not to abort.

This is not to say, however, that a woman and her partner who is party to the decision should enter into it without a lot of careful and thoughtful consideration. There probably was a good reason why that soul requested passage into the human experience through her, and this has to be honored. One has to consider whether the reasons for saying 'No' are really good enough to support that decision, given the opportunity being presented for both mother and future child. One has to consider all sides of the argument before making the decision.

But the prospective mother has a soul too, and her soul's wishes need to be honored as well. After all, we have free will and sometimes that freedom is exercised by saying "No" to a soul who is asking to incarnate through that soul's body.

I do think, however, it is important that the woman says "No" as early as possible after discovering that she is pregnant. Notwithstanding the fact that none of us know when the attachment actually happens, I can imagine that the more strongly the soul's energetic vibration has attached itself at the physical level, the more difficult it will be for it to detach and return home.

When you do the forgiveness worksheet or one or more of the online programs, use the above approach when you come to the Reframe, and make sure you don't include any guilt or shame. Write a letter to the soul to whom you said 'No,' explaining how you felt and why is was not appropriate for it to come through you at that time. Wish it well. Tell it how much you loved it and hope that it found another woman to incarnate through. Do this, even if you think it probable that soul may have come through later as one of the children you had subsequently, or suspect it may be a friend's child you feel very drawn to.

POSTSCRIPT: To complete the explanation of the Radical Forgiveness Ceremony, I should explain that when people have walked the circle in response to all of the questions that apply to them, everyone gathers around while I read the story of the *Little Soul and the Sun,* by Neale Donald Walsch. This leads us in the direction of the Radical Forgiveness Reframe, but we anchor this fully into the body by having them go back into the circle while we read out the same questions again, but this time adding a tag line about seeing the perfection in whatever was the situation.

In the case of the abortion question, we say: *"If you ever had to agonize over, or be party to the decision, whether or not to have an abortion, **and yet you are willing to see the perfection in the situation,** walk the circle."*

This time, however, they find a partner on the way over and say, *"I honor your willingness to see the perfection in the situation."* They almost all walk and report feeling a whole lot better for doing so, as well as experiencing a definite shift in their energy.

The Radical Forgiveness Ceremony is something anyone can learn to facilitate and we offer a resources-rich kit entitled "The Radical Forgiveness Ceremony-in-a-Box." It includes all the information you need to be able to share this healing event with others.

RESOURCES FOR THIS APPLICATION:

(Details in the Resources Section at the
back of this book and at www.radicalforgiveness.com.)

Worksheets:
Radical Forgiveness Worksheet
Radical Self-Forgiveness/Self-Acceptance Worksheet

Package: *Radical Forgiveness Ceremony-in-a-Box*

---

25 Practical Uses for Radical Forgiveness:
Solving the Problems and Challenges of
Everyday Life in a New Way

PART SIX

Applications for Transforming
Mass Consciousness

Application #24:

Transforming the Illusion of Tragic World Events

It can be very good spiritual practice to make a point of exposing oneself to the pain and suffering of some 'awful' event and doing one's best to remain open to seeing the perfection in the situation.

Nothing challenges our willingness to entertain the possibility that there is Divine perfection in absolutely everything more than watching the news on TV and seeing a whole string of terrible things occurring out there in the world. Wars are continuous. People torture others and commit awful atrocities. We hear of the rape, abuse and denigration of women everywhere, the sexual exploitation and abuse of children, the degradation of the environment, corruption and crime, etc. We could go on and on listing such things that we find so upsetting and difficult to reconcile with the concept of Radical Forgiveness.

I have to say I would feel very despondent indeed about human beings and life in general if I didn't have the idea that there is some kind of perfection in it all from a spiritual perspective, and that this perfection will someday be revealed to us as the only true reality. Without Radical Forgiveness, I would have very little hope for humanity.

Because our perception of spiritual reality is so limited, we simply cannot fathom how it can be purposeful in any spiritual sense for such things to happen. It's beyond our comprehension, given our level of conscious awareness at this time.

Another way I deal with this dilemma is to observe that when we have events in our own private lives which make us feel like victims, things always seem to change for the better if we use the Radical Forgiveness tools. Even if we use them in a way that simply helps us fake-it-til-we-make-it, it still works. I then say, well, if it is true at that level, then it must be true in all circumstances, no matter how bad things appear to be.

The principle here is that Radical Forgiveness cannot be selective. It either works for everything or nothing. There is no in between. If it works at the level of my own experience, then it must also be operative in exactly the same way when it comes to the larger events. My own consciousness is simply too limited to be able to see it clearly.

That's why we need the tools. They help us to fake-it-til-we-make-it, using our own Spiritual Intelligence to connect to the higher truth of what appears to be happening. This is the part of us that can see the bigger picture and yet chooses, for its own reasons, to keep it hidden from us – at least for now.

In order to give some kind of left-brain hook to hang this all on, I go back to my model of the soul's journey. The first phase comprises a journey of learning and discovery about how it feels to be separate while being spiritually unconscious. Then comes the awakening, and then the second phase during which we expand into Love.

Using the principle of 'as above – so below,' I apply the model to the group soul of the entire human race. As a species, we seem to be approaching the breakdown that always precedes the awakening. Hopefully we will soon be waking up. In Application #25, I explain how we can assist in making this shift happen.

Again, we have a worksheet that helps us to energetically transform the upsetting events we see happening in the world. I recommend you use it every time you are confronted with something bad 'out there.' It will help you maintain your willingness to entertain the possibility (notice I don't say belief) that it's all part of a Divine plan, even while you feel compassion and empathy with and for the people involved and take action to help alleviate the suffering.

When we do lend a hand in a practical way, we are much more powerful if we do it with a consciousness that is free of the need to blame or add to the pain by getting angry and upset. If we remain willing to see the hand of God in the situation, we will, simply by virtue of our vibration, be of much greater value that we otherwise would if we were angry.

Many people who consider themselves spiritual make a virtue out of avoiding the news on the grounds that it is too negative. I have some sympathy with that idea, if only because the news can be so distorted. The fact is that reported events are only negative if we remain blocked off from the idea that there is a spiritual purpose being served by them.

It can be very good spiritual practice to make a point of exposing oneself to the pain and suffering of some awful event, while doing one's best to remain open to seeing the perfection in the situation. That's why I recommend you keep the Radical Transformation Worksheets handy, and use them when you see something on the news that is really upsetting.

This not only helps keep your vibration high, I feel certain it helps raise the collective consciousness as well. It also contributes to the improvement of the actual situation in a profound way. Even while you sit in your armchair watching events unfold on the other side of the world perhaps, you will be making a difference. You really are that powerful. The worksheet follows on the next page.

The Radical Transformation Worksheet

Applying the Technology of Radical Forgiveness to World Events

1. What is happening in the world now that disturbs me is:

_____

_____

_____

2. My feelings about this situation are:

☐ Fear ☐ Anger ☐ Helplessness ☐ Apathy ☐ Panic
☐ Anxiety ☐ Aloneness ☐ Hopelessness ☐ Abandonment
☐ Betrayal ☐ Despondency

Other feelings _____

3. I am noticing my automatic human reactions to this situation include: ☐ Laying blame; ☐ Punishing those responsible; ☐ Doing something about it; ☐ Changing something; ☐ Complaining, ☐ Being right ("I told you so."); ☐ Screaming; ☐ Fixing it myself; ☐ Demonstrating; ☐ Declaring war; ☐ Getting revenge. ☐ Other: _____

(Make some notes about the ones you checked and any others that come to mind.)

_____

_____

_____

4. If I had infinite power and authority over the situation, I would . . . *(Fantasize as much as you like and don't censor your thoughts. If you think people are to blame, include any and all dark thoughts that might be running through your mind.)*

---

5. In spite of my initial feelings of (as in 2)

---

and my initial automatic reactions of (as in 3).

---

the action that I can take that might make a practical difference is to . . . .(e.g. send money, go help, write a letter; become a whistle blower, protest, etc. It may be nothing.)

---

6. What I know for certain I can do that will make a BIG difference energetically is to read out loud the Radical Forgiveness Invocation, plus the proclamations that follow.

<u>**The Radical Forgiveness Invocation**</u>

May we all stand firm in the knowledge and comfort that all things are now, have always been and forever will be in Divine order, unfolding according to a

Divine plan. And may we truly surrender to this Truth whether we understand it or not. May we also ask for support in consciousness, in feeling our connection with the Divine part of us, with everyone and with everything, so we can truly say and feel – we are ONE.

7. Having read the above Radical Forgiveness Invocation, I now realize that what is occurring is perfect. It is all part of the process of moving from a consciousness based on fear and greed to one based on love and harmony. **By holding the vision of a 'healed' world, I am making a huge contribution to having the shift happen relatively quickly and easily.**

8. I hereby declare that I am willing to hold this higher vibration, and to resist all temptation to react to events with fear and despondency. Whenever I feel myself slipping back into fear, I am taking six deep breaths in order to bring myself back to my center and maintain my vibration. I am centered now and have released the need to continue feeling what I was feeling in #2 above. *I choose peace.*

9. I now realize too, that what was happening 'out there' was a reflection of what needs, or needed, to be healed in me. What it may be mirroring for me is, or was:

_____

_____

10. By forgiving the situation in #1, I have automatically forgiven myself. I am grateful for the healing.

287

11. I am centered now and have released the need to continue feeling what I was feeling in #2 above. I choose peace.

Signed:_____ Date: _____

RESOURCES FOR THIS APPLICATION:
(Details in the Resources Section at the back of this book and at www.radicalforgiveness.com)

Worksheet:
Radical Transformation Worksheet
Radical Forgiveness Support Group

Application #25:

Surviving and Riding the Shift: Trusting the Process

I have left this one until last because it is the one that, while perhaps the most challenging and even disturbing, could in the end be the only one that matters. It concerns how Radical Forgiveness will help us ride the coming shift in consciousness, the shift many people feel has already begun.

F or as long as we have been on this planet, we have been evolving spiritually. It has not necessarily been a smooth journey. We have gained and lost our spiritual bearings many times, and have gone through long dark periods as well as days of enlightenment.

But we always keep evolving towards a higher order of awareness. In our own lifetime we experienced a significant shift in consciousness and a raising of our vibration, even if we didn't notice it. This occurred in 1987, during the 'harmonic convergence,' when there was a powerful vibration hitting our planet and us as a result of a number of planets being in a particular alignment with Earth.

There is now a deeply felt expectation among people in the world that a much bigger shift in consciousness is just around the corner. We shall move from our current reality, based on fear, separation, pain and suffering, to a reality based on Love, Harmony and Oneness. However, it is also expected that the shift will be preceded by an extended period of chaotic breakdown, dramatic climate change and a total collapse of all existing financial, legal, governmental and social structures everywhere.

The financial crash of 2008 might have been the beginning of the breakdown and at the time of writing it appears likely that it could happen again. How this will play out we don't really know. But if it goes according to all the prophecies about this age in time, we could soon be witnessing the death of the social order as we know it, and the birth of a wholly new way of living and being. The long experiment with separation will be over.

For such a breakthrough to happen, the breakdown of the old order and the world view that has supported it has to happen. It's the equivalent of a healing crisis, and in that sense will be perfect and all part of the divine plan. The question is whether you will be able to see it that way and hold that higher vibration, even when things get really bad. Or will you, like the majority, be drawn back down into fear and despondency?

Not everyone will choose to go with the change. Many will resist the change, and the degree of that resistance will determine how difficult and cataclysmic the transition will be. This is why it is so important to begin preparing for it immediately by doing the work to raise your vibration. You want to maintain the Radical Forgiveness perspective, no matter what is happening. It is also why we have created a membership organization so that those of us who are awake will have the knowledge and tools necessary not only to survive, but to be proactive in actually facilitating the shift.

If and when the necessities of life to which we have become completely accustomed and taken for granted suddenly become very scarce (like a steady supply of food, water, fuel, transportation and other consumer goods), and the structures on which we have always relied to give continuity, predictability and order to life, begin to crumble (like the financial system, the legal system and perhaps even government as we know it), we will need the full range of spiritual tools that our Radical Forgiveness approach provides.

They will help us move through the experience with relative ease. We will also want to engage people in the conversation, giving them the awareness of what the choice is, then provide them with the spiritual technology to make the choice possible.

Radical Forgiveness will help you to stay awake, enabling you to move through the experience with a knowingness that everything is in divine order, regardless of how it may appear. The Radical Forgiveness worksheet, whether online or on paper, will be an extremely helpful tool for shifting energy when there is time to reflect and spend the time doing it. The 13 steps audio tool will still be perfect to listen to when you are at home or in the car, assuming that you still have fuel to run a car!

But the tool that will be most immediately helpful will be the 'Emerge-n-See' 4-Step Process. Once memorized, it's instantly available exactly when needed. And it works.

If and when such crisis times do actually hit, large numbers of fearful and confused people will probably not be easily persuaded to take the time to learn about and use the Radical

291

Forgiveness worksheet. However, they might, in their anxiety, be willing to reach out and grasp at something as simple as the 4-Step Process, if only to see if it worked. I believe it will work for them even if they have never heard of Radical Forgiveness, because it will resonate something deep within them and they will feel a sense of peace when they do it.

My hope is that this book will help to create a mass awareness of the fact that such a simple tool as the 'Emerge-n-See' 4-Step Process can help people get through the difficult times ahead and emerge with a transformed consciousness. My vision is that you, already having this awareness, will learn the 4 steps by heart if you haven't already done so, and will find ways to teach it to others.

If people seem deaf to it now, they won't be when everything around them is breaking down. They will come to you because they will notice that you are not in fear like everyone else, and that you always seem to know what to do. That's because you will be receiving guidance, assuming you are in a peaceful enough state to receive it.

Here, again, are the four steps:

1. Look What I Created! *(Accepting that you are the creator of all circumstances in your life, and that there is a purpose in all that is happening.)*

2. I Notice My Judgments and Feelings But Love Myself Anyway. *(Acknowledging your humanness through awareness of your feelings, judgments and thoughts.)*

3. I Am Willing to See the Perfection in the Situation. *(The Radical Forgiveness step.)*

4. I Choose Peace.

At the moment of the Great Awakening, we shall see the emergence of humanity into a world of Oneness and the ultimate merging of heaven and earth - a truly joyful vision - but getting there will be a big challenge. Holding that vision when everything is breaking down will be difficult especially if we have not practiced it in our lives beforehand.

The Radical Forgiveness strategy that comes into play in this regard is **Radical Transformation.** (See Application #24.) This strategy is specifically designed to give you practice in applying the technology of Radical Forgiveness to any and all disturbing events that happen out there in the world - things like airplane crashes, tragic accidents, tsunamis, murders and so on.

Its purpose is to help you first feel the fear, or whatever other emotions you might feel initially. You then transform those feelings by being willing to entertain the possibility (notice I don't say belief) that there are no accidents. It's all part of a divine plan. When you do this, you transform the energy and begin the healing process.

Doing a Radical Transformation worksheet on world events will not only keep your vibration high but will help raise the collective consciousness as well. It will also contribute to the improvement of the actual situation itself in a profound way. Even while you sit in your armchair watching events unfold on the other side of the world, you will be making difference if you hold it that there is perfection in the situation.

I believe that by using the Radical Transformation tools, taking specific steps to raise your vibration, and settling into an acceptance of the new paradigm in advance of the breakdown, you will be of great assistance in making the coming shift in consciousness a relatively smooth one, no matter the circumstances. Now is the time to expand your consciousness in the direction of Love.

Maintaining a high vibration will also enable you to receive guidance about where to go, what to do and how best to facilitate the shift. If you are in fear and despondency, you will not be in a state where you can hear the messages given to you by your own spirit guides, guardian angels and others in the angelic realm.

They are all standing by, ready to assist in creating this wonderful vision of heaven on earth. Radical Forgiveness is a form of prayer and a request for help in maintaining a willingness to see the perfection in any situation, and the angels do respond. They will help you, but you will need to be in a state of being where you can hear their whispers.

Now is certainly a great time to be on the planet as we anticipate the shift and observe how it unfolds. I hope it will be in my lifetime, but if am called to the other side beforehand, I shall be of service from there to smooth the way for those who remain to make the shift happen. Even if I am not here, I trust this book will be instrumental in easing the process in some way for others.

RESOURCES FOR THIS APPLICATION: (Details in the Resources Section at the back of this book and at www.radicalforgiveness.com)

Worksheets:
Radical Forgiveness Worksheet
Radical Transformation Worksheet

APPENDIX 1:
Available Resources

The following resources are exclusively those that have been mentioned in one or more of the 25 Applications for Radical Forgiveness published in this book. Some are free while others may be purchased. Details of each one can be found on the website, www.radicalforgiveness.com or by scanning the QR Code. Instructions on how to download and/or purchase them are provided there also. Books can, of course, be purchased in any bookstore and through Amazon.com. They are also on Kindle and available as eBooks downloadable from our website. I trust you will find these resources helpful.

BOOKS: The following books are mentioned as recommended reading in several places in this book.

• *Expanding into Love: A Handbook for Awakening to Who You Are, Raising Your Vibration and Creating Enlightened Relationships.*
• *Radical Forgiveness: A Revolutionary Five-Stage Process for Finding Peace in Any Situation.*
• *Radical Forgiveness: Making Room for the Miracle eBook.*
• *Radical Self-Forgiveness: The Direct Path to Radical Self-Acceptance.*
• *Radical Manifestation: The Fine Art of Creating the Life You Want.*
• *Spiritual Intelligence At Work: A Revolutionary Approach to Increasing Productivity, Raising Morale and*

Preventing Conflict in the Workplace. (Includes Hidden Agendas at Work.)
• ***Hidden Agendas at Work:*** *The GiCo Story.*
• ***Why You Still Need to Forgive Your Parents*** *And How You Can Do It With Ease and Grace.*

WORKSHEETS
• Radical Forgiveness Worksheet
• Radical Acceptance (of another) Worksheet
• Radical Self-Forgiveness/Self-Acceptance Worksheet
• Radical Transformation Worksheet
• Radical Manifestation Worksheet
• Radical Self-Acceptance Worksheet
• Money Consciousness Worksheet

The Worksheet Technology
The potency of these worksheets should not be underestimated. They are simple to do and yet they achieve amazing results. This is because they activate your Spiritual Intelligence which is the 'mind' of the Higher Self. This part of you knows the Truth about you and the perfection of what is. It perceives you doing the worksheet as a cry to be connected with that Truth and it will respond accordingly. That's why I call doing the worksheet 'secular prayer.' However, your body is your antennae for your Spiritual Intelligence, so it really helps the process if you speak it all out loud so your body feels the resonance of the words. It also helps you feel the power of the words and stops your mind becoming involved to the point where you merely skip over them.

It is our observation that you cannot just do this form of secular prayer in your head. It simply does not work. That's because it becomes an intellectual exercise which only activates the rational mind, not the mind of the Higher Self. This is why we lay such stress on doing the worksheets and encourage you to push through the resistance to doing them, which is something we all feel. Our ego doesn't want us to heal, so it creates all kinds of resistance.

All of the above worksheets are FREE and available for download from www.radicalforgiveness.com. However, we also have created online interactive versions of most of them, and these are only available to those who are members of *Colin's Cafe* membership site.

AUDIOS
The 13 Steps Technology
We realized there was a need for a process that was very similar to using a worksheet but one that would be quicker and even easier to use. The 13-Steps Technology was the answer. It is, in effect, a verbal worksheet. You simply listen to a list of 13 questions and respond verbally to them with a resounding YES! This is perfect as a follow-up process after having done a worksheet just to make sure the energy has been fully dispersed. It is also less likely to be hijacked by the mind because the words are received aurally, and you have to use your voice to respond. This activates your Spiritual Intelligence, so make sure you say Yes as loud as possible so your body gets the resonance of it.

- *13 Steps to Radical Forgiveness*
- *13 Steps to Radical Manifestation*
- *13 Steps to Radical Self-Forgiveness*

Other Audios
- *Radical Forgiveness 3-Part Audio Set. (Additional to the book)*
- *Radical Forgiveness Meditations Audio*
- *Karen Taylor-Good, Singer/Songwriter, Audio*
- *Radical Forgiveness Chakra Meditation & Etheric Cleansing Meditation Audio*
- *The Wake for the Inner Child Meditation*
- *Radical Self-Forgiveness Practices Audio Set on CD (Additional to the book)*

VIDEOS
- *Cancer & Radical Forgiveness Video*
- *Self-Forgiveness Audio/Video*

WORKSHOPS
While all the self-help tools and methods of doing the work result in significant shifts in energy, and in many cases cause one's life to change dramatically, there may come a time where you feel the need to join a group healing experience in order to get the result you want. The ones mentioned in this book, and fully explained on our website, are as follows:

- *Manifesting Your Perfect Mate Workshop*
- *Radical Forgiveness "Miracles" Workshop*
- *Expanding in Love Workshop*

ONLINE PROGRAMS
- *"Breaking Free"* A 21-Day Online Program for Forgiving Your Parents
- *"Family Matters"* A 21-Day Online Program for Forgiving Your Siblings

- *"Great Expectations"* A 21-Day Online Program for Forgiving Your Kids
- *"Moving Forward"* A 21-Day Program for Forgiving Your Partner
- Radical Grieving Online Program
- Radical Self-Forgiveness/Self-Acceptance and Releasing Toxic Secrets 3-Part Online Program
- Radical Manifestation Online Program
- X4 Radical Money Online Program

PACKAGES
- QEMS 'Q' Kit of Tools
- Awaken Your Soul at Work Combo Pack
- Radical Forgiveness Ceremony-in-a-Box
- Tipping Method Radical Weight Loss Online Program

Use the coupon code **2USES** during the checkout procedure to receive $5 off your first order.

301

APPENDIX 2:
The Radical Forgiveness Support Group

It is very hard to hold the higher vibration on your own all the time. For that reason, we need the loving support of people who will rescue us from Victimland, and help us return to the truth of who we are by connecting us back into the higher vibration. It gives us somewhere to go on a regular basis, and like-minded people who will remind us of our commitment to be in the higher vibration; and, if we have temporarily lost our connection – due to a personal upset or what is happening in the world – to bring us back to that commitment. We can feel confident that any time we go into our victim mode, they will lovingly point this out and help us see the perfection.

This is very different from a normal therapy support group, the usual purpose of which is to support you in your story, keeping you in victim consciousness. Friends, relations or colleagues who do not understand the new paradigm and/or have not yet awakened are not able to help us either, for the same reason.

The Radical Living Support Group works well if you stay within the guidelines and keep to the structure. It falls apart if you don't. The meeting itself should last no longer than an hour. Social time comes after, if at all.

GUIDELINES

• No Appointed Leader
It is very important that no one person is leader. Whoever has

the highest vibration that evening should ideally be the one to lead. With a permanent leader, there will be times when his/her vibration is low and it would be unfair to them, and everyone else, for them to lead. Once the group has aligned its energy by reading the invocation, the group simply waits for a leader to come forward. Someone will say, "I feel like leading tonight." It does not matter who, because the agenda is always the same, and it is written down for the leader to follow.

• No Giving Advice
Giving therapy or advice is **NOT** the purpose of the support group. If the facilitator, or any group member, attempts to give people solutions to problems, they should be gently and lovingly reminded of this rule. *(This is probably the most difficult guideline to stick to, but it is the most important. If we try to solve problems or give explanations, we make them real and give them power. The Radical Living tools simply dissolve problems.)*

• Commitments
Our commitment is that we will not support anyone in their story or their assessments about what is occurring. We will listen openly, lovingly and without judgment, but we will not "buy in" to it or give it energy, because we know it is only an illusion. Our commitment is to support the person as they shift out of the story into the knowingness of Radical Awareness – that what is happening is quite different from the apparent circumstances, and is purposeful in the Divine sense. The means to creating this shift is to do one of the 13 Step processes; Radical Forgiveness; Radical Self-Forgiveness; Radical Acceptance; Radical Transformation. Whichever one

we use will create the necessary energy shift. That will also release the blocked energy that has, in all likelihood, caused the upset in the first place.

• The Priority is the Emotional Check-In

This is item number three on the agenda and is always to be considered the priority. Even if this takes the whole hour, and nothing else happens, the commitment is always to give this kind of support to all who need it. Typically, however, it is usually just one or two people. The facilitator for the evening goes around the group asking each one to rate, on scale of 1-10, how strongly they need to do the 13 Steps that evening. Someone who is a 10 is obviously someone who is extremely agitated and in victim mode, whereas someone who is a 3 or a 4 might be marginally upset, but not unconscious or in Victimland, and, therefore, not in dire need of rescue.

The facilitator then asks the one with the highest need rating, *"Which of the 13 Steps processes would you like to be taken through?"* (More often than not it will be the Radical Forgiveness process.) Once that is established, he/she will ask the person, *"Who would you like to take you through that process?"* The person will tend to choose someone whose energy is just right for that person at that time.

The process is carried out by the person chosen. The rest of the group simply brings all their attention to the moment and projects love and support to the one going through the process. (They should not go through a parallel process for themselves at the same time. If they need to do it, they should ask for their turn.)

• No Discussion

At the end of the process, there is no comment or discussion of the situation, either then or during the social period after the meeting if you have one. Talking about it would only destroy the energy field created by the process and it would be neither loving nor supportive.

Then the facilitator goes to the person with the next highest need and repeats the process. This goes on until all who need to have done it. The facilitator then decides how to use the rest of the time — if indeed there is any. It is often the case that by the time one or two have done a process, the ones who were 5 or under have come to a place of peace simply by being in the love vibration and no longer have any need to do the process.

• Success Stories

The next part of the meeting is an invitation for people to share success stories. These are stories where it has become obvious that an energy shift has taken place as a result of being in the higher vibration. The most likely stories people will share are the effects of the 13 Steps process they experienced during the previous meeting. This is NOT the time to share events in our lives that are not related to the effects of living the awakened life-style. Those can be shared in the social time afterwards.

• Asking for Support

An important aspect of the meeting is when members ask for vibrational support. The request is made in terms of what the person needs to feel or affirm, relative to spiritual principle, in order that their energy shifts with regard to the difficulty.

If, for example, a person is having financial problems it would not be appropriate or self-supportive to request donations! The request should be made that "*please support me in feeling completely abundant and in knowing that I always have all that I need and feeling grateful for that.*" The group agrees to hold that vision of support for that person for the whole week. They might also encourage the person in this particular case to do a Radical Manifestation Worksheet.

The group then anchors that vision of perfection and total abundance by first rubbing both hands together to stimulate energy movement, and then holding their palms toward the person. In unison they say the following affirmation:

"*John, we unconditionally love and support you just the way you are, in all your power and magnificence. You are a spiritual being divinely guided in all your thoughts, words and actions.*"

• The Positive Reflection Exercise
If there is any time remaining, a nice way to complete the meeting is to do the positive reflection exercise. The quickest way is to break into groups of three, and each one says to the other two, "John, the beautiful, wonderful qualities I see that you reflect back to me are:" (Then speak those out - 2 or three words is enough.) Then you close the meeting.

• Time Agreement
Make an agreement on time, and make it firm and meaningful. When the group has aligned energetically, begin the meeting on time. People who have created being late should honor the group energy by entering softly into the meeting, and

silently. Never wait for a latecomer. Consistent latecomers should notice their resistance to being there on time as a way of withholding love from themselves and others. In the following meeting, they can ask for support in feeling high intention to receive and give support. Do not support people in being habitually late. It breaks the energy of the group to have people coming late, and you would not wish to support them in a habit which is self-sabotaging.

• Stick to the Rules and the Given Format
As I said in the beginning, this support only works if you adhere strictly to the format and to the rules. It is, in essence, an experience in shifting energy in the most efficient way — simply by using the tools that are specifically designed to shift energy (the 13 Steps processes), and by aligning with spiritual principle and the energy of Love.

• A Closed Group
It should always be a closed group since it becomes a very safe place to come and share. If numbers are low, and I think 6-8 is ideal, you might allow members to suggest people they know who might like to join. You would only want people who were very familiar with the Radical Living Strategies and who were committed to living it.

• Frequency of Meetings
We have found that to meet every two weeks works best. Once a week is too much, and once a month is too long and leaves people feeling unsupported.

Format for RF Support Group Meeting:

1. Align the group energy by reading the RF Invocation together.

May we all stand firm in the knowledge and comfort that all things are now, have always been and forever will be, in Divine order, unfolding according to a Divine plan. And may we truly surrender to this Truth, whether we understand it or not. May we also ask for support in consciousness in feeling our connection with the divine part of us - with everyone and everything - so that we can truly say and feel we are One.

2. Allow a facilitator to 'emerge' for that evening.

3. *Emotional Check-In.* Each person says how they are feeling and then, on a scale of 1-10, rates their need to experience the 13-Step process on a particular issue.

4. *Processing:* The person going through the process nominates who shall read the questions for them. Everyone else focuses their healing energy on the person experiencing the process, holding thoughts of oneness, unconditional love and connectedness to Source. *(Remember, there is no discussion or comments after the process.)*

5. *Success Stories:* Members share specific examples of how Radical Forgiveness has been working in their lives since last time. *(Request that they be as concise as possible.)*

6. *Requests for vibrational support*: Some people might need help in framing their requests for support in terms of what they need to *feel* or *affirm*. This helps us tap into the Spiritual

309

Intelligence that will take us beyond our apparent difficulties. (Anchor it energetically by saying together: *"N____, we unconditionally love and support you just the way you are, in all your power and magnificence. You are a spiritual being divinely guided in all your thoughts, words and actions."*

7. Formally close the meeting and confirm time for the next meeting.

END OF PROCESS

APPENDIX 3:
The Career Opportunity

If you feel your life's purpose is making a difference in the lives of others, and you love to share information with others, here's a way to fulfill your dream. Showing people how to apply Radical Forgiveness to their every-day lives and live a spiritually awakened life is enormously satisfying.

We have several online training courses to choose from depending on your previous experience and your desire. You may see yourself becoming one of the following:

1. Radical-Living Coach
No previous qualifications are required but it is an ideal "Advanced Program" for existing Life Coaches.

You will be qualified to share with clients the principles and use of the four main Strategies for Radical Living:

1. Radical Forgiveness
2. Radical Self-Empowerment: (Includes Radical Self-Forgiveness and Radical Self-Acceptance.)
3. Radical Transformation
4. Radical Manifestation

In addition to coaching individual clients as they learn to use the relevant tools for each strategy, you'll be trained to personally mentor people through the Online Radical Manifestation program. And it doesn't stop with individual coaching: you will also be trained to run classes, Radical Living Support Groups, PowerShift Groups, and seminars.

2. Radical Living Master Coach

This takes the Radical Living Coach Program to the next level of mastery in coaching people in the Strategies for Radical Living, and includes the opportunity to present workshops. The only qualification required is satisfactory completion of the Radical Living Coach program.

3. Radical Forgiveness Therapy Practitioner

If you are a certified and licensed practitioner in the field of mental health and would like to add Radical Forgiveness Therapy to your clinical practice, then this course is for you. It is designed on the assumption that you already have the necessary skills in working with people on their basic life issues and able to do emotional process work with them. Depending on where you practice and what board you come under, this course may be eligible for CEUS.

4. Energy-Body & Chakra Clearing Practitioner

The is an ideal course for massage therapists, reflexologists, Reiki practitioners and others who wish to extend their repertoire of skills and expand their career. Even if you are not one of the above, you can still benefit from taking this course. You will learn a method of instantly dissolving negative energetic patterns likely to be active in the subtle bodies and each of the seven chakras in your client's body. Now available as Home-Study or Online. 8 CEUs are available with this program.

5. Book-Study Leader and 'Satori' Gamemaster

Running a book study group and introducing people to the 'Satori' Radical Forgiveness Game is very rewarding and both are fun ways to share the work with other people.

Go Here For More Information

For more details about these programs, including the cost, money-back guarantees and payment plans, scan the QR Code to watch a video on your mobile or go to http://www.radicalforgiveness.com/training-coaching/ to view the information.

APPENDIX 4:
Colin's Café — A Membership Site

I t was in the summer of 2012 that we created Colin's Café. The idea was to create community based around the Radical Forgiveness philosophy and as a way to support people making use of the tools that make it work in everyday life.

The first thing we put on the menu then, exclusive to members, was all of our renowned and well proven online interactive tools. We wanted them to be there, available 24/7, to enable members to gain mastery over every aspect of their lives by using them regularly. (Some are reminiscent of the free tools you already know about, but because they are online and interactive, they are many times more powerful.) They are:

The Online Interactive Tools Exclusive to Café Subscribers

• Radical Forgiveness Online Interactive Worksheet
• Radical Self-Forgiveness Online Interactive Worksheet
• Radical Transformation Online Interactive Worksheet
• Radical Manifestation Online Interactive Worksheet
• Emerge-N-See 4 Step Process to Find Peace Instantly
• Radical New Career Manifestation Program
• Radical Wealth Retrieval Program
• Relationship Assessment Questionnaire
• Radical Reconciliation Worksheet
• Manifesting a New Relationship Worksheet
• My Boundaries Worksheet
• Radical Acceptance Worksheet

The Online Audio 13-Steps Processes Exclusive to Café Subscribers

- 13 Steps to Radical Forgiveness Process
- 13 Steps to Radical Self Forgiveness Process Audio
- 13 Steps to Radical Transformation Process Audio
- 13 Steps to Radical Awareness Process Audio
- 13 Steps to Creating Funding for a Project Audio
- 13 Steps to Radical Weight Loss Audio
- 13 Steps to Creating a Job Audio
- 13 Steps to Radical Empowerment Audio

In addition to having 24/7 access to all the above Online Tools, we included on the menu some exciting live activities. They are:

• **The Reading Room.** This where I take a section of one of my books, and read a part of it. I then invite you to ask questions or share a comment with me and your other friends in the tea shop via our online community discussion area.

• **Three 8-day Online Courses** that give you a firm grounding in each of the Radical Living strategies; Radical Forgiveness, Radical Empowerment (which includes self-forgiveness and self-acceptance), Radical Transformation and Radical Manifestation.

• **Access** to the archives of all my articles, blogs and podcasts, so you can delve more deeply into the topics that interest you most.

The membership fee is minimal and you can set it up to be paid monthly or annually. And you can cancel at any time, no questions asked, of course.

I am sure you will enjoy being part of a community in which all the members are excited by Radical Forgiveness and who use it regularly as part of their Radical Living lifestyle.

To join go to http://www.radicalforgiveness.com/colins-cafe/ or scan the QR Code.

BIBLIOGRAPHY

Application 1:
Walsch, Neale Donald., Frank Riccio, and Neale Donald. Walsch. *The Little Soul and the Sun: A Children's Parable Adapted from Conversations with God.* Charlottesville, VA: Hampton Roads Pub., 1998. Print.

Application 2:
"Antidepressant Use in the UK | Opinium Research LLP." *Antidepressant Use in the UK.* Opinium Research, 12 Feb. 2011. Web. 25 Sept. 2013.

Wehrwein, Peter. "Astounding Increase in Anti-depressant Use by Americans." *Harvard Health Blog RSS.* Harvard Health Publications, 20 Oct. 2011. Web. 25 Sept. 2013.

Application 3:
Lipton, Bruce H. *The Biology of Belief: Unleashing the Power of Consciousness, Matter and Miracles.* Santa Rosa, CA: Mountain of Love/Elite, 2005. Print.

Application 4:
LeShan, Lawrence L. *Cancer as a Turning Point: A Handbook for People with Cancer, Their Families, and Health Professionals.* New York: Dutton, 1989. Print.

Application 5:
Sheldrake, Rupert. *A New Science of Life: The Hypothesis of Formative Causation.* Los Angeles: J.P. Tarcher, 1981. Print.

Application 8:
Luber, Marilyn, and Francine Shapiro. "Interview With Francine Shapiro: Historical Overview, Present Issues, and Future Directions of EMDR." *Journal of EMDR Practice and Research* 3.4 (2009): 217-31. Print.

Application 12:
"ICT Statistics." *ICT Statistics.* International Telecommunication Union, 15 July 2008. Web. 29 Sept. 2013.

"Statistics/Data." *Statistics/Data.* National Center on Elder Abuse (U.S. Dept. of Health & Human Services), 2009. Web. 29 Sept. 2013.

Application 13:
Gettleman, Susan, and Janet Markowitz. *The Courage to Divorce.* New York: Simon and Schuster, 1974. Print.

Application 22:
Levine, Stephen. Unattended Sorrow: Recovering from Loss and Reviving the Heart. Emmaus, PA: Rodale, 2005. Print.

319

About the Author

Born in England in 1941, Colin Tipping was raised during the war and in early post-war Britain by working-class parents. He has an elder brother and a younger sister. By his own account his parents were good people, loving and hard-working, and he considers himself blessed by having had a stable and enjoyable childhood in spite of the social hardships of the time.

Even as a boy, he seemed to inspire the trust of people who needed to talk about their feelings, they finding in him a person who would listen to them and not judge. After a four year stint in the Royal Air Force, and three years in the corporate world after that, he became a college professor, but even then often found himself being sought after to provide counseling for people.

He emigrated in 1984 to America and shortly thereafter became certified as a clinical hypnotherapist. He was not religious then and still feels "free" of any organized religious dogma. His spirituality is essentially practical and down-to-earth, simple, free and open-ended.

In 1992, he and his wife JoAnn, whom he met in Atlanta and married in 1990, created a series of healing retreats in the North Georgia mountains for people challenged by cancer. In recognizing that lack of forgiveness was a big part of the causation of cancer, they set about refining a new form of

forgiveness which later was to become what is now recognized as Radical Forgiveness. In 1997, he wrote the book *Radical Forgiveness,* and began doing workshops in January of 1998. He now has an Institute for Radical Forgiveness in the U.S.A., Poland and Germany that offers professional training to those who wish to be certified to share this work.

He and JoAnn spend several months of the year in Europe doing lectures, seminars and workshops. He is in demand as a keynote speaker at conferences and his work is praised by many of the best known and respected people in the field. He is the acknowledged authority on the healing of individuals, couples, groups and corporations through the methodology of Radical Forgiveness.

In 2004 he turned his attention to the corporate world where he perceived a need that could be satisfied by a version of Radical Forgiveness that would be appropriate for, a corporate culture. He could see how it would raise productivity, increase morale and increase profits. He wrote and published *Spiritual Intelligence at Work* in July of 2004 to lay down the rationale for that and has since been consulting with organizations on how to use the Tipping Method to great effect.

His book on relationships, *Expanding into Love,* published in 2013 is receiving wide acclaim and supports a lot of what is in this book.

Colin has three children from a previous marriage and ten grandchildren, all living in the U.K. He has no plans to retire.

CPSIA information can be obtained at www.ICGtesting.com
Printed in the USA
LVOW04s0101151214

418843LV00030B/980/P